Jacob Boehme's Songs of Enlightenment

Jacob Boehme's Songs of Enlightenment

Poetic Wisdom for the Spirit and Soul in Commemoration of the Four-Hundredth Jubilee of the Theologian's "Now I Go Hence into Paradise" (November 17, 1624)

JONATHAN CLOUD

RESOURCE *Publications* · Eugene, Oregon

JACOB BOEHME'S SONGS OF ENLIGHTENMENT
Poetic Wisdom for the Spirit and Soul in Commemoration of the Four-Hundredth Jubilee of the Theologian's "Now I Go Hence into Paradise" (November 17, 1624)

Resource Publications
An Imprint of Wipf and Stock Publishers
199 W. 8th Ave., Suite 3
Eugene, OR 97401

www.wipfandstock.com

PAPERBACK ISBN: 978-1-6667-8547-0
HARDCOVER ISBN: 978-1-6667-8548-7
EBOOK ISBN: 978-1-6667-8549-4

09/20/23

I WANT TO BE YOUR PLAY-FELLOW

I want to be *your* play-fellow—
Be my humble surrendered soul—
I'm the Almighty's *inspiration*,
Gentle breath of God,
Holy *anointing*
purifying you
to be the Holy Spirit's Temple—
Searching vast *Adonai's* depths
I'll teach you all things
more precious than rubies,
finer than gold my gain—
I'll be your precious *Pearl*,
Beauty more glorious than the Moon,
Virtue more sovereign than the Sun,
immaculately conceiving
true Wife of your youth,
your never-failing comfort be
in all afflictions,
Balm for all sores,
Cure for all diseases,
Sure antidote against death—
I want to be *your* play-fellow—
I ask no more than this—
To be *your Joyful Companion*,
Ever assured guide,
never to forsake you,
but your safe convoy
through this world's wilderness
into the *blessed Paradise*
of our perfect *Bliss*—

Contents

CONTENTS

Contents

Poem Summaries

POEMS OF THE INTRODUCTION

LILY

A Good Friday, Falling—on the soul's utter surrender to God's love-will

My First Mother—a paean on the divine *scientia*, or insight-knowledge

The Wind—a quiet reflection on the eternal and temporal natures

The Rubied Cicada—on the soul's immortally sacred nature

My Dear Virgin—of the soul's rejoicing at receiving Christ's Body, Noble Sophia

Hot Love Oil—on the genesis of the soul before the foundation of this second creation

What Grace Is This?—on the spirit-soul's mystical call and baptism

Hertz Is the Flash: *Feuerblitz* I—of the will spirit's first fleeting glimpse of eternity

Lovely, Gentle, and Still—praise to God as the soul dives down into the *Mysterium Magnum*

He Shoots Up as a Lily—on how reason should place its confidence in the Christ

Spark—The spark of faith pierces the five senses while sinking into God's abyssal love.

Surrender, Falling—the soul's thanksgiving as it is immersed in the depths of grace

Flee Nakedly—a reflection on the first early Good Friday morning

Fruitful Rain in Your Still Mother—In the Father's maternal bosom is our rest.

Carmel Pacific *Gelassenheit*, March, 1972—a reflection on sinking down into the oceanic depths of God's love

Shooting Forth Bright Into the Fair Lily—Our fellowship is in Christ, the Tree of Life.

Descent Into the *Rakiya*—on the primordial Firmament's mystery of immersion grace

Blade—on the austereness of holy desiring

Delight Draw Me—a chuppah song of the soul's sinking down into God's *delight*

Out of the Heart of Darkness—on the nature of the human will-spirit's rebirth

LILY-ROSE

Blossom in the Time of the Lily-Rose—the theologian's blessing on the readers of this section

Nights, Zion Downtown—on the secret ecstatic dancing of being possessed by the Holy Spirit during illuminated speaking or writing

Once When I Was Yours—a chuppah song of the soul's yearning for her beloved Christ

The Widow's Walk—Our soul is invited to watch with the theologian as he peers into the Depths.

You Know This Love Well—a reflection on "Once when I was Yours"

Eagle: *The Inspoken Ungrund*—a spontaneous song of abyssal transfiguration

The Hinge—on the imaginative desire in the soul's *will-spirit* for life or for death

No Mere Angel—The enlightened soul stands on the Earth, engaging in spiritual warfare against its former rulers, Satan, and his host.

Married to a Beast—the soul's loss of Divine Sophia, and her restoration in Christ Jesus

Stand Before the Crib Where Jesus Is Born—our need to seek for the *Barmhertzigkeit*

Feuerblitz II—on the joyous flash of lightening, or magic fire

Know Thyself: *The Enemy Within*—of the corrupted aspect of human nature, and how we should learn to rule over it

Burning Cold Night—on the cosmological origin of the human spirit's darkness

Pregnant—on how the will-spirit and soul are corrupted by *imagining* into nature

Forked Lightening: *Feuerblitz* III—on the freedom of the will-spirit to choose light or choose darkness

This Rose Is Not a Rose Except—on the inspired or inbreathed grace of God

As I Lay Upon the Mountain Towards Midnight—The Virgin of Wisdom and Love comes to the aid of the struggling soul and pledges it her troth.

Miserere—of the soul's patient endurance with the succor of the Virgin's Love

Pure Understanding Moon—four benefits of true fasting

Bright Lily—on the coming of the Champion to liberate the spirit-soul from sin

Signless—on the crisis bringing the soul to *metanoia*

Know Thyself: *The Wild Heifers*—We should awake from sleep and be aware of God's love for us.

Sapphire Dawn—Wisdom teaches the soul how to hear Christ's Voice.

Tender It the Love—The enlightened human spirit prays in the Holy Spirit for its struggling soul.

A Terror of Great Joy—sanctification of the human spirit by a removal of its dark dragon

Most Holy Sweet Power—a most efficacious three-line prayer to purify the darkest of hearts

Lydia's Song—a chuppah song on "such a measure of grace to fulfill my hunger"

Fire in the Iron—on ardently seeking the true Kingdom of the Heavens within

Rocking in the Cradle—We should go forth out of sleep-inducing Babel-like religion.

Mother of Pearl—on the hidden dynamics of being born again

Pure Child—on the purification of the spirit and soul

PEARL

Magus—For thy honor, Lord, I openly set forth this Pearl.

Pearl—of the Virgin Wisdom's gift of herself to her beloved soul

Mary—on the dynamics of why all peoples are enjoined to call Mary blessed

You Became Man for My Soul's Longing—a chuppah song of spiritual espousal

Golden-Silver Child—on the *likeness of God* in Man juxtaposed to *God's image*

We Were Once Men and Women—on the harmonious androgyny of the spirit-soul's true body united to the Christ

Except for the Fair Paradisical Rose-Garden—on our eternal and androgenous body

The Seraphic *Kadosh* of Wisdom: *A Food to the Divine Fire*—the holy song igniting the fire of divine Wisdom

My Being Is Your Moving in the Heavens—on the transfiguration of our spirit and soul

The Body Beautiful—Our fleshly body of death is replaced by Christ's Wisdom body.

Adam of the Crystal Sea—Christ's death clothes the soul with the *eternal element.*

I Was Embraced With Love—The theologian speaks of his illuminated gift of writing.

Rose Garden—a chuppah song of the fruit-bearing union of the soul and its Virgin

One Love's Majestic Shining—of how God's pure love overwhelms the painful self

Star-Dust—on the essential body of the *Over-Soul*

Dancing With Sophia—an introduction to the *Inspeaking* meditation practice

Stand Still With Your Face Towards Me—a chuppah song of noble Sophia's desire for union with the soul

The Time of the Lily—an invitation to the *Dancing with Sophia* or *Inspeaking Practice*

Riding in the Chariot of the Bride—an encouragement to all who have received the gift of wisdom, but are timid, or ignorant about dancing with Sophia

Intimate and Indigenous—a further proposal for the *Inspeaking Practice*

That by Which God Saw and Heard in You—preliminary incentive toward the practice

The Fellowship of His Sweet Interceding—a basic practice instruction

The Thousandth—on the benefits of the Wisdom meditation practice

Magia—the imagination and the *magia* during the spirit-soul's purification

Iridium: *The Magical Begetting*—restoration of the Virgin Sophia to the soul by Christ

The Crystalline Silver Temple—on Man's true body hidden within our animal-like temporal body

Beloved Companion—the redeemed spirit-soul as Mary in Christ's Virgin Wisdom

The Yield-Light Constant—a song of the nature of the eternally present *Yield-Light*

The Doe—on the permeation of all nature by the *Yield-Light*

The Enchanted Bumble Bee—on the true body's Resurrection into life upon the transformed Earth

Upper Cross—on the divine and most holy anointing oil

You Have Clothed the Naked—an introduction to "Jupiter Sparkling Springing Up"

Jupiter Sparkling Springing Up—on the motion of the quintessential Word of divine power (*Yield-Light*) activating and tincturing physical nature

The Chambered Nautilus: *Coming to the Limit*—of the beatific union with Christ's Virgin Wisdom body, when the soul leaves the animal body at death

The Pearl Is in the Jewel—ardently seek the Holy Spirit's gift of Wisdom

Noble Burning White—a spontaneous song of transfigurative joy

These Great Moments: *On the Rebirthing of the Human Spirit*

Fire of God's Love Draw Me—on looking forward to the Judgment at the Last Day

How Fair Now the Pines of Lebanon—a wayfarer's song of homecoming

Set This Heart on Fire—a prayer for the will's hardened heart to be inflamed with the love of God

Pray Naked—on the true Christian *apatheia*

High Life: *The Night Watch*—on watching and praying during the predawn

JEWEL

Love You Take All: *To the Noble Virgin*—on the all-sufficiency of God's love

Out From the Very Heart: *A Mandala Shield*

Soul Food—on eating the flesh and drinking the blood of the Son of Man

Outspoken—on the divine illumination

The Teacher—on the enlightened soul's healing ministry to Christ's *Body*, the church

Come Forth Gently—concerning the anointed apostolic speech

If Only My Spirit Did Sit in Your Heart—on the necessity of the azure faith to inform the heart unto God's hope and love

The Scent of Wild Roses: *Reply to Arnold's Dover Beach*

This Covenanted Heart—on the restored human spirit as the true temple of God

These Crimson-Bruised Petals—the restoration of all things through Christ's wounds

The Wood Chuck—on the supra-imaginal interfacing of the eternal and the temporal

Not Suspected Suddenness: *Feuerblitz* IV—an eight-year-old lad's vision of the salvific glance of eternal light in a darkened mind

Venus on No Half-Shell: *The Gates of Love*

This Pure Craving Ours—When the soul becomes pregnant, the spirit gives birth.

Fair and Fiery Sunday—The prodigal returns to his beloved Father, the Most-High.

Falling Into the Blessed Birth of Love—a longing of the will-spirit to pass into God

Unbound—on the ministry the Virgin Sophia entrusts to the chosen soul

They Shall Not Hinder—dedicated to the Little Flock belonging to Lord Jesus

Pledge Your Own Heart: *A Paean to the Holy Spirit*

Swift as a Pure Thought Magical—on the divine infinite *Punctum*

This Terrible Consuming—on God's jealous love for our soul

The Crickets—the Immersion Grace on early Holy Saturday morning, 1973

Anemone—a look at the Paradise in Dickinson's "Summer for thee, grant I may be"

The Oriole's Song—The soul sings of the Love which created it in God's image.

I Thee Endow—The Christ-like soul renews his pledge of fidelity to Virgin Sophia.

Verse Epilogue: For the Lily's Sake—on why the theologian has written his illuminated works

Acknowledgments

I AM GRATEFUL TO my ever-faithful wife, Sophia, who has provided a creative haven in which to write. Also, I am thankful to my dear son, Justin Cloud, without whose teaching patience and computer tech expertise, I could never have transferred the poetry to an online state nor navigated the publishing process.

Thank you to the educators, my dear eldest son, Caleb Petrin, and his loving wife and mother, Julie, as well as my grandchildren, Joseph and Jane. Though you are far away, your love has always been felt.

Thank you, my dear daughter, Sarah Dawn Petrin, humanitarian with heart and hands to serve the poor, homeless, and disenfranchised throughout the world in a selfless manner.

Finally, thank you Wipf and Stock for accepting this first book. Especially, the gracious patience of Emily Callahan (editorial staff), and the timely assistance of marketing manager, Joe Delahanty, have been of inestimable value.

And all praise to the tenderly loving Father of Our Lord Jesus Christ, who has redeemed this sinner through his Heart-Son's precious blood of his love shed on Golgotha.

Abbreviations

A	*The Aurora*
EG	*On the Election of Grace*
EP	*The Epistles of Jacob Boehme*
FQ	*The Forty Questions of the Soul*
	CL Clavis (The Key)
IN	*Of the Incarnation of Jesus Christ*
MM	*Mysterium Magnum*
FT	*Four Tables of the Divine Revelation*
SR	*The Signature of All Things (Signatura Rerum)*
STP	*Six Theosophic Points and Other Writings*
STP	*Six Theosophic Points*
SMP	*Six Mystical Points*
MP	*Mysterium Pansophicum (On the Earthly and Heavenly Mystery)*
TS	*Theoscopia*
TFL	*The Threefold Life of Man*
TP	*The Three Principles of the Divine Essence*
WTC	*The Way to Christ*
OTR	*Of True Repentance*

TR	*Of True Resignation*
OR	*Of Regeneration or The New Birth*
SL	*Of the Super-Sensual Life*
WDI	*The Way from Darkness to True Illumination*
WTC	(CCEL) *The Way to Christ*
OTR	*Of True Repentance*
OR	*Of Regeneration*
TR	*Of True Resignation*
SL	*Of the Super-Sensual Life*

Introductory Poem

A CORAL TREE GROWS IN GORLITZ

A Coral Tree grows in Gorlitz—
Seed and scion of the holy Tree of Life
on the Western side of the Crystal River
spreading its roots into the *Ungrund* soil—
Bright scarlet blossoms flaming
proclaiming the Morning Redness of the rising Dawn,
whose sap of brotherly love unfolds its healing leaves
of Lord Jesus' *Holy Love-Spirit* of Life,
each bough and twig being bound to the other—
Eternal joy compassionate in them flowing
at its *spirit*
Sweet nightingale's
holy evensong:
Merciful I AM
emerging Moon stay—
End all strife—
Your blossoming Light
in all things living, moving—
Barmhertzigkeit
through all beings springing
yet possessing nothing

save that whose will dies
possessing that you must
with your streams of Life
embracing desire's delight
and pour out no more
your mulled wine
of jealous wrath
at Sin's Night,
its numbing sleep—
Only fan your bright fire
of this God's exceeding
precious gift to Man—

Introduction

The Poetics, Practice, and Compleat Theology of the Theologian of Fire

Jacob Boehme's Songs of *Enlightenment: Poetic Wisdom for the Spirit and Soul* is a hand-held looking-glass into the illuminated lyrics of the Holy Spirit, flowing from the pen of the Gorlitz shoemaker. These verses came forth spontaneously, while the versifier studied the rich Restoration English translations of the works of Boehme. Yet life could not be breathed into each particular chosen text without midwifery. The lyrical children were given birth to only after the seraphic *Kadosh* of Wisdom (*TFL* 10.28; Isa. 6:3; Rev.4:8) began to be daily intoned.

Each versification's impulse unfolded in its own place and timing, with pretty much a mind of its own. This pen just seized the opportune clear looking-glass, when the particular song decided to make itself known, to emerge and display its brilliant colors. And the highest of them were complete surprises sprung unaware, when, as it were, the back was turned. That is, there was no perceptible conceptual intent toward the context of the passage being read. For this reason, the Holy Love-Spirit placed a restraining order on this hand's urge to write a separate explanatory reflections section for the poems. Therefore, any true intuition, or reflection, must occur between you, the reader's own essential mind, and the poem alone.

Yet, despite this rational self's often clumsy interference, the by-product of the labors began to bear fruit. And also, often was the case when a particular primary passage, which bore the seed of the poem, was so prolix that, once the joyous silent beauty began to emerge, my spirit was stunned. For this heart, and this hand, just so easily drew each of the illuminations out of the ground of its marmoreal context.

> Write, my quill—
> Draw out this inkwell
> no ebony, but
> light Divine—
> One-only Will,
> this Harmony
> *Infinity* beheld—

In consequence of the above, dear reader, let us together share in this pilgrimage to these illuminated treasures, hidden right within the hearth of even our own spirit-soul. For the true quest does not actually take us far afield to locations like Jerusalem, Mecca, Mt. Athos, Varanasi, Bodh Gaya, or Rome, or even our own local house of worship of brick, wood, and stone.

Lord Jesus teaches the Samaritan woman at Jacob's Well that the heavenly Father seeks worship in spirit and in truth. The true seeking, and true finding, occurs within one's own spirit and soul, once re-illuminated as an inner Zion. This is the divine Finger on the pulse of our own original self, our own personal sometimes joys, and often times great afflictions. However, it requires the awakening of a Mary of Bethany, one who out of love and grace intuitively knows how to choose the better part, quietly at Messiah's feet.

With this disposition of being empty of our own preconceptions, let us as well take our seat beside the Theologian of Fire, this servant of the Master's servants. But before we do, let the reader also remove her or his acquired rationalistic shoes. So shall we together be enabled by that indefinable *Barmhertzigkeit*, or wisdom and love, to step forward, and stand on such consecrated ground.

For only then will these verses gleaned from his texts bestow warmth, and light, and vision.

For these teachings, of which the versifications are mere drops, uniquely bring fire mingled with their waters. And this dynamic is far from being a superaddition to the normal Christian walk by faith through the grace of Lord Jesus. Rather, just standing beside the Crystalline Sea allows one to hear the harps of God resonate from the sound of its gentle ebb and flow. It is here that the theologian beckons mere spiritual children to the banqueting table.

> I only sought *Jesus Christ*, the pleasant Love-Heart,
> myself from the majestic wrath of God to hide—
> Through the foolish the Most High's counsel abides,
> thence it may be known that his Hand alone imparts—
> So, in my works into the *heart of all beings* go with me
> into such as surpasses all the wonders this world brooks,
> all things scarce deciphered in a thousand books,
> find real satisfaction of mind—from those masked sounds
> be freed—
> Such high joy to *know God*, so able to see and find *all things*
> for the precious Philosopher's Stone lieth therein—
> Seek and find, knock to open,
> for herein radiates the *Pearl* hidden—
> Therefore, if into your hands come my writings,
> I would that you look upon them as a child's
> in whom the Highest hath his work *scriven*—
> Therein is couched that which no reason may apprehend,
> unfolding to the illuminate so easy, so plain and mild—

Therefore, here is *not* just one of numerous theologians, who gives light to our intellect. Rather, his corpus has been touched by the divine fire of primordial Wisdom [*Prajnaparamita* Skt., *Sophia* Gr.]. In this sense, Boehme's spirit-words come to our minds with most of the rational dross removed. And if we are not blinded with the cataracts of an intellect, void of an abiding faith in the *most holy sweet power Name Jesus*, with patience silver, then pure gold, and sometimes precious stones may be discovered in their luminous depths.

This then is why such intuitive insights [*prajna* Skt.] can only bring *turba,* or disturbance to those of us who have not yet had our persona drawn into the *cross-birth,* and then rebirthed out of the matrix of one's spirit [*pneuma* Gr.]. For the painful source is its soul [*psyche* Gr. pron. su-hay], still raw with the eternal nature's fire of the first three forms alone. It is from out of this raw and lightless conceptual mind's angst that contemporary so-called "scholarly experts" cry "opaque!" "abstruse!" "confounding!" and "never read these days!" in order to discourage potential seekers. These would wave their *ignis fatui* before the eyes of the simple children in faith, hindering the reading of the holistic Boehme. For it is in the context of his Christian-based cosmological economy, and guidance in the Holy Spirit *alone,* that we are disentangled from the dark web of humanistic rationalism. And it is the latter path most commonly taken, the lemming-like herd mentality, which circumvents the will-spirit's holy desiring of faith, springing up into *God is love.*

Hence, the simple child-like faith approach in reading *The Way to Christ, The Incarnation of Jesus Christ,* as well as the theologian's other more formidable works, is mirrored in an ancient parable. It is like a great, deep, and wide river, which large animals, as elephants and such, must swim across with might and main to reach the other shore. However, little creatures like wood mice and marmots, when crossing over the same river, merely walk across, barely getting their paws wet. This is why the theologian never flags, throughout his texts in constantly reminding the readers, that only those who by a free will have become as *the Father's little children* can begin to fathom the depths of these teachings.

Otherwise, with the power of reason alone, without the illuminated grace of faith, these concepts begin to take on fantastic and bizarre Kafkian-like forms. Again, they appear as an ever-shifting kaleidoscope, or warping figures, such as one would encounter upon entering a house of mirrors at the carnival. This is why, even at the very beginning with *The Aurora,* the theologian often holds up a "restricted text warning" for those ubiquitous intellectual window-shoppers.

However, if this little book has found its way into your hands, and has already begun its work of magical attraction, viz., drawing motion of God's love on your spirit, then rest assured that the flaming sword barring your entrance in has been removed. Please enter into the hidden anointing that accompanies the text. Go slowly. Go mindfully. For the quiet deep resounds at the sound of the deep grace and mercy [*Barmhertzigkeit* G.]. It beckons you to attend the Voice of the One who desires to share these illuminations with you, whom he has called to this *right juncture*. And when just one word, a line, or a couple of lines of any particular poem has drawn you in, then *stop, stand still, savor*. That is enough for this Day. Afterwards, never forget to seal with thanksgiving to the tenderly loving Father *in the Name Jesus*, or a praise of *Kadosh*. This is in order that the pure gift you have just received will not leak out the vessel of your heart.

In conjunction with the above, it is crucial to understand that the *compleat theology* informing each verse, is in no manner the fruit of this poetaster's "teeming brain." Rather, all is pure Holy Love Spirit illuminated Boehme, yet often tinted with my own English language mind-set, and Americana life experience metaphors. Examples of these are the doe resting beneath the willow tree, the *Yield-Light* tamed marmot emerging from its Kennebec River lair, the Taiwan lotus, the Louisiana cicada, the white sands of the Carmel, California Beach, hitch hiking through the Nevada Desert, and so forth. This is in order to paint portraits for myself, just as much as for the reader, of eternal verities that are often expressed by the theologian in abstract phrasing.

However, our Jacob is never short on his own unique metaphors: the lily, the lily-rose, the cat warily circling round the hot kettle of stew, the heifer balking at the freshly painted stall gate, the Tree of Life, the way-fairing pilgrim searching for home, the lyre, the dark hand rocking the cradle, and his favorite, the rose-garden, and many others. Nevertheless, one should be very careful not to confuse metaphor with existential reality. For when Boehme writes of the divine Virgin Sophia as being the bride of the bridegroom, viz., the *born from above* holy soul, this is an exact portrayal of eternal life in our union with the *one body* of Jesus of Nazareth, the Messiah. And true wisdom here is knowing the difference between metaphor and universal truth.

Furthermore, in order for you, the reader, to plumb the meaning of these verses in depth, you may want to source their references. In order to facilitate such a study, you should be familiar with the simple referencing layout of this book. First, all sources may be found in the bibliography. This Boehme *exclusive* bibliography comes from the public domain Jacob Boehme//University of Pennsylvania Online Books Library. Carefully note that the title spellings are quite detailed and often archaic. This is because the online site often contains a number of editions of each work, ranging from the late 17th Century through the early 20th Century, with especially the former having their own non-standardized forms of spelling. Therefore, our bibliography spells out the exact titles which this writer employed for the poetry. Once you have found the correct online entry, then just follow the particular "Link" listed, which is most often an American university library.

Additionally, an Endnotes/Sources section is placed just before the bibliography. In this sources listing of the four sections of poetry, the abbreviated title of each exact book, treatise, or letter (epistle), and its specific chapter(s), and paragraph numbers (added by the 17th Century translators for convenience) that each poem employs, are listed. Please pay especial attention to *the first* work, chapter, and paragraph numbers listed, as they are normally the initial text from which the poem was drawn. Then again, it is in each of the references listed that even the simplest person may verify whether the versifier was faithful to the theologian's illuminations.

Continuing on concerning the dynamics of reading this volume, if the Holy Spirit has magnetically drawn you to these poems, in the love of God please chant the sacred *Kadosh*, or Seraphic Song of Wisdom. Whether singing it quietly, or spontaneously dancing at the *presence of the Holy Ark to you*, its protection and creative light is a nexus from which your spirit may blossom. And it can be exquisite when with devotion it is chanted in the Hebrew.

However, with a heart-felt love of God, and compassion for the destitute, the stranger, and the lowly, chanting the *Holy, Holy, Holy* in your own native tongue can be just as efficacious. For the Most Holy peers into the heart, rejecting all lip-service, and taking to his tender-love bosom even the child, who can only barely stutter it. So if possible, learn to intone the *Kadosh* in Hebrew, especially the initial *thrice Holy to the Lord of Hosts*. For whether in Hebrew, or your mother tongue, it will seven times enhance the intuiting of these poems to your spirit-mind's essence, illuminate your path in the love of God, and foster a compassion for lost souls.

Furthermore, the *Kadosh*, whether chanted aloud, or allowed to sink down silently revolving in your mind, is efficacious in spontaneously pulling the soul's fire into the *Inspeaking Practice*. The presence of the anointing will draw your soul into its *revolving luminous spirit*, which your bride, divine Sophia, united with *Christ in us*, has occupied as her temple. Standing still, and turning, you will see her there, not by conjuring up an idea of her by imagination. Rather, you will recognize her by remembrance (even like you could your own mother's face, even in a vast sea of people) of how she was united to you, when your soul was betrothed to Lord Jesus during *the View*. This was, and is, the warm light of the Father's love flowing into his *Express Image*, and your own true pristine self, being even *as he is*. Yes, this is the Third Day. First, in relationship to the Anointed One, your spirit-soul has become the Lamb's bride. Secondly, in relationship to noble Sophia, your soul has become her beloved bridegroom. These two facets of the pearl are a great mystery, further enhanced by the third, that is, our simultaneous *eternally being Mary in the Covenant of Grace*.

Then with these ineffable mysteries of the Christian faith etched in our minds, let us consider the intent of this poetic collection. First, it unfolds the hidden beauty of the theologian's wisdom *directly from his texts alone*. This method frees it from the above mentioned ever-prevalent scholarly secondary source books and articles. For almost four-hundred years (especially in the last fifty years) these counterfeit currencies have merely sashayed around the banquet, without daring to directly address the theologian's visionary and holistic soteriology, or his in-depth dynamics of the human soul and spirit. For Boehme's inscrutable intertwining of these with a compleat, viz., perfect in its quality, and unsanitized Christian cosmogonic paradigm, *is even now, and is to be,* the constant lighthouse for the church in the world during the Third Millennium.

Therefore, secondly, a catharsis is initiated in which to release the Theologian of Fire's illuminated Christian theology from those shadowlands of philosophical and gnostic isms foisted upon it by, as Boehme himself designates them, *the Antichristian churches in Babel.* And in doing so, as seen below in his "The Firm Articles of the Christian Faith," these diamond teachings of pure and simple faith are reset in the relief of their proper Judeo-Christian milieu.

Third, the viable *Inspeaking* Christian Practice, or *Dancing with Sophia,* which Boehme himself privately employed, and then writes about for the well-being of the church (but has from the beginning been obscured and forgotten), is here for the first time unearthed and partially unfolded. This nonmeditation, or better, *recollection of familiarity,* percolates just beneath the lines of this whole collection. Yet, it doesn't surface until the appearance of its own signature poem, "Dancing with Sophia," the first of seven specifically on the practice.

This silent practice, most often referred by the theologian as *Riding in the Chariot of the Bride,* finds its Tibetan Buddhist equivalent in the *Trekcho* nonmeditation of Dzogchen, or *Atiyoga.* Here the Christian, by an act of faith, turns the soul into the splendor in the face of Christ abiding in her or his essence of mind, or illuminated spirit [*pneuma* Gr.]. For our Savior, the Son of Man, manifesting his virgin birth, shed blood on Golgotha, and resurrection from the dead, has incarnated among us surrounded by his Virgin Body of Wisdom. This is the nothing more precious than the pearl in the jewel, viz., virgin image of the splendor of God's love hidden beneath the jewel of the eternally abiding theological virtues of faith and hope. This is the same mind of the Christ, our own mind essence [*tincture*; *Rigpa* TIB.] awakening and blossoming out of the once truncated spirit's heart of darkness.

Here, it is crucial that the reader should not be confused, especially concerning this familiarity with one's primordially androgenous self. For one's true face, or mind of Christ, which is in us the hope of glory, is introduced only because of the purification of a seeker's soul. Her or his spirit [*pneuma* Gr.] is, subsequently, luminously clothed by the words which Lord Jesus speaks to them during the *Agape Feast* (Mt.18.19-20). When this occurs, at one particular time and place, *we become even as Mary is in the covenant of grace*, as she intones the *Magnificat*.

And this recognition of our eternal spirit-soul as Mary in the covenant of grace, looking into the face of Virgin Sophia, is due to our once for all having become refamiliarized with the lost *Imago Dei* during the glance, or *kensho* [JP.]. Now the nonmeditation to follow this awakening glance, called the *Inspeaking Practice*, is not a form of Shamata mindfulness meditation, Centering Prayer, Chan Buddhist pre-*kensho* zazen, or Christian Zen. Rather, these are all methods of various traditions, preparatory to the View, designed to calm the mind from disturbing emotions. For it is easier to see all the little fishes, swimming along the bottom of the clear pond, if the wind is not disturbing the surface of the water.

Each of these extra-Christian techniques can, in their own spiritual milieu, be helpful tools to calm the non-stop conceptualizing mind. However, they cannot be that one smooth bridge spanning the troubled waters of our confused nonlife of thought. In other words, all these forms of meditation are preliminaries, and so, incapable of bringing the *born-from-above* Christian's *inner spirit* (but never the fleshly outer man) to holy perfection, even as our heavenly Father is both holy and perfect.

For the continuous state of Lord Jesus, Son of God, and Son of Man, was, in the days of his flesh, one of dancing with Sophia, viz., his own divine body, brought from the Father's maternity. With this his cherished body, he planted his church on this Earth. Born again souls, made holy by *grace through faith*, can, if they choose, participate in the same dancing or *Inspeaking*. The one and only prerequisite is that the Christian has had to, according to the numerous promises and promptings of the Holy Spirit in the Scriptures, *perseveringly asked the Father in Jesus's name for his gift of divine Wisdom*. And if you have persevered in asking with a sincere heart, then at one time and place God fulfilled that holy request, breathing on and anointing you from above in his Wisdom knit together with Love. *If* the reader has so requested and then received, then you can never ever forget or be doubtful of that consecration and choosing. It is the consummate *axis mundi* of one's own life on Earth, unspeakable, unexplainable.

And now, O blessed reader, if you have asked of the holy and tenderly loving Father, and received, *not for any other gift, or for that ubiquitous glossolalia*, then I shall here mention a few simple things that you should not forget. And the seminal word is "Remember." Dear soul, take your mind and go back to those sacred moments, and *recall* the intimacy of the third pouring out, the pouring out of love that is greater than all. That was when you were willing and longing even to instantly leave this your body of flesh, your soul and transfigured body so joyfully desiring to pass though death, now being in perfect union with *the flesh of* Lord Jesus.

Now here, dear child of God, simply put, is the practice: *Remember*. And then in your intimate recalling, place your very mind's eye into that stream, into that gentle flowing *even as it has never ceased*. Recollect the unspeakable joy, as you, *being both Mary and her adopted child* (as was John the Apostle), gaze into the wondrous eyes of your loving bride, the wife of your youth, Sophia. Then if you can remember just this betrothal of ineffable union, and place yourself once more even for a few moments into this eternal dynamic, then that is the practice. Nothing more needs to be done. Stand or sit still, after intoning the sacred *Kadosh* in order to more readily draw your mind into this wedding dance with your bride. Then letting go of that sacred spoken name of divine wisdom enkindling the fire of love, enter into the bridal chamber, into this foretaste of the Marriage of the Lamb.

Just simply recall, recollect, remember and gently plunge once more, again and again into the stream of your mind essence [*Rigpa* TIB.], the luminous mind of Jesus, even as you once knew it so intimately. And for encouragement and help in this practice, study carefully the theologian's *Supersenusal Life*, as well as "The Gates of the Paradisical Garden of Roses" in *Of True Repentance*. Both tractates are in *The Way to Christ,* and are its only complete studies in the Boehme corpus. The former text speaks of various details, like the benefits of the practice, how long should you should maintain a dance session, and so on, while the latter is an affective encouragement to persevere in this dance.

While considering these invisible things of faith, the true reader should be wary of the numerous gainsayers. Such persons can only guffaw at the thought of an Introduction to the View of one's *true face* as being the luminous mind of Lord Jesus, the Messiah, and afterwards practicing just that. The blind leading the blind would have enlightenment as something restricted to Sufism, Buddhism, Jainism, or Hinduism. This fallacy, established on ignorance, is put to rest in a pithy statement of the Buddhist master, H.H. Jigdal Dagchen Sakya Rinpoche, who founded the Sakya Monastery for Tibetan Buddhism in Seattle. He was the same teacher who ordained this Christian poetaster of Jacob Boehme's compleat theology as *Ngakpa Yeshe Rabgye*. In 1984, the rinpoche and his students bought what had been a Baptist Church building in order to remodel it into a Tibetan monastery. During the initial renovations, some misguided students wanted to have a stained-glass window in the sacristy, of Lord Jesus being baptized in the Jordan, torn out. However, Sakya Rinpoche turned to them, and said, "Leave it there! Tibetan Buddhism regards Jesus as a great *Bodhisattva*."

With the above verities etched in our minds, a well-known Indian parable is here apropos. It is the story of a destitute farmer with a large family. One night in a dream, he was told by a voice that in order to find a great treasure, all he had to do was go to the king's palace. There he would find the treasure at the threshold of the royal court. Immediately, he left his farm, and travelled the far distance to the royal city. However, upon attempting to enter the great door into the king's court, he was stopped by a giant armed guard. The farmer said to the guard, "Please let me pass! For I was told in a dream that I would find my treasure here." Then the guard looked down at the farmer, and laughed, saying, "Ah! Just last night I also had such a strange dream. And it was that a farmer dreamed that he had a treasure in the king's court yard, and then travels all the way here to find it. But what the farmer didn't realize is that 'the king's palace' meant his own humble house. And 'the threshold of the king's court' meant that the treasure was buried under the floor, right in his own hearth!"

Yes, the treasure lies well-hidden right beneath the very hearth of Lord Jesus, the Heart-Son's own *ecclesia*. However, come and see the anti-Christ spirit, the one antagonistic to the recognition of God himself become a man in the flesh. And *in his most holy sweet name Jesus,* his grace is powerful to bring complete enlightenment to our spirit-souls. It is the same spirit of anti-Christ, which has successfully buried this treasure hidden away for so long, that almost all of Christianity is not even aware of its existence. And the Holy Love-Spirit of Lord Jesus sends to humankind special messengers, such as Jacob Boehme and Jeanne-Marie Guyon, to both teach about and directly show how to receive *a pointing out* or *recognition of the View.*

Nevertheless, these messengers, due to the same envy that made both the primordial cherubim with one-third of the angels rebel against God, and the Sanhedrin demand that Jesus be crucified, have become martyrs (messengers sent from God as witnesses) *in the church.* As rare in the Christian West as stars shining at noon, yet these messenger-witnesses are post-haste branded as "heretics" by that same ubiquitous covetous greed which permeates church prelacy.

Therefore, for the above noted reason, a biographic excursus into the anomaly of being both a Christian and a *Ngakpa,* or ordained non-monastic practitioner of *Dzogchen,* is in order. During the night of Good Friday, 1973, and following morning, Paul Reynolds (1952–2003) of Gardiner, Maine, and myself were *in the Presence* [*Rakiya* Heb., *Sherab* TIB.]. This is prescribed by Lord Jesus as where two or three are gathered in his name, or *Agape Feast.* And while we were studying with progressive *insight* the Gospel according to John the Apostle, the writer received the Baptism in the Holy Spirit. He was anointed *from above* with the sacred gift of wisdom. The former was the first edge of the two-edged sword of the word of wisdom [*prajna* Skt., *sherab* TIB.], *first* cutting away all dualistic thinking. Then the other edge, this same wisdom [*jnana* Skt., *yeshe* TIB.], opened her threefold eye to reveal the mind of Christ in the face of Lord Jesus, as the original mind and face in the Image of God.

Here, let us back up a year before, early winter in 1972, Portland, Maine. The writer was invited to a private reading of the *Bardo Thodol* [TIB.] or *Tibetan Book of the Dead*. And though he had never even heard of this text, yet the bit of Kazi Dawa Samdup's translation that we listened to was strangely fascinating. There was no person present in the group even remotely qualified to comment on the text, so in awe we were simply attentive to the *terma*. However, only twenty-five years later did the realization of the connection between first listening to the *Bardo Thodol*, which promises a glimpse of enlightenment, and the soon to occur anointing with the gift of wisdom on Good Friday, 1973, fall into place.

Now let us go still further back to the well-spring of the above two events. It was the summer of 1956 in the small salt mining village of Jefferson Island, Louisiana, where the Cloud Family, with two girls and two boys in elementary school, lived for three years. For our father, Barnette Cloud, worked there in the Diamond Salt Mine. My brother, Barnette Jr., was eight years old, and I, a year younger. Early that summer, our mother, Willie Lee Cloud (*nee* Thompson), requested that her two sons be baptized (the daughters, Elizabeth and Deborah, being considered still too young according to the Bible Belt ethos) at the Abbeville Baptist Church, due to their confession of faith in the Lord Jesus Christ.

Later that summer, after the two Cloud lads had been immersed *in the name of the Father, the Son, and Holy Spirit*, I began to have an inscrutable yearning to ask Lord Jesus for the gift of his wisdom-and-love [*agape* Gr., *caritas* Lat.]. For in my child's mind, these two seemed to be one and the same. However, God is

Merciful, in that he hid a fact from the kid who wasn't particularly fond of girls. It is that the true unsurpassable Wisdom is the feminine *Sophia* in all the Greek texts of both the Old and New Testaments, as well as the feminine consort, *Samantabhadri* [SKT.], in Vajrayana Buddhism.

The way I approached my Lord and Master was like any shy country boy would have. I would wait until towards late afternoon, after the four children were finished playing in the woods, across the horse shoe bent road from our rented small white clapboard house. Once Mama's voice sounded from the porch to come wash our hands for supper, instead of goings with the others, I would stay behind in a small designated clearing. For there in an oak tree I had placed a small cross, hastily formed of two twigs, bound by a short twine-like section of thin vine. It was in this secret place to which I repaired, that the recently baptized child knelt on the ground before the cross in the tree, and fervently implored the Lord and Savior for his wisdom-love.

And somehow this child had, from his mama's words and from Sunday School lessons, grasped the truth that one should earnestly pray and not faint, at least until the Holy Father answers your request. Therefore, every late afternoon for three weeks or more, the same routine occurred, that is, Mama's calling the children to supper, with my staying behind to kneel before the cross in the oak. There I kept crying out to Lord Jesus for his wisdom and *agape*-love, and wouldn't let go until an assurance was received. And then one day, the promise of "prayer without fainting" was fulfilled. During a late afternoon, while on my knees crying out, suddenly a clearly confirming interior Voice whispered, "Yes, Jonathan, I have heard your prayer, and I will give you your heart's desire."

However, *Adonai Saboath* is pleased to bestow, as a light shining in a dark place, his first promised horizontal white flash of lightning (*Feuerblitz* G.) as a sign of confirmation. In this manner, he gently comes to all those who have entered the new birth, through faith's confession of the *most holy sweet power Name Jesus*. This is as an irrevocable initial sign, or mark upon the spirit, even though this light that shines in the darkness of the soul is rarely consciously recognized. For it was only a few months after the clear answer to the lad's prayers, that Lord Jesus Messiah confirmed his covenant of grace to his servant's soul. This is poetically rendered in "Not Suspected Suddenness: *Feuerblitz* IV."

Now moving forward to over fifty-five years later, and entry into old-age, the once bright-eyed and determined boy, stumbled upon a shocking truth regarding Lord Jesus's church in the world. Why did the Holy Trinity, enigmatically, begin to initiate God's promise of the bestowal of wisdom and love through the spark of Padmasambhava's *Liberation Through Hearing in the Bardo*? It is due to the same church, bought with Christ's blood on Golgotha, having completely abandoning that precious divine knowledge and love. In the same manner that Israel, in the age of her prophets, had given herself over to unabashed idolatry, the church in the world for many centuries has also been playing the role of Hosea's unfaithful wife, Gomer.

And at least, from the time of Adonai Sabaoth sending his rejected messenger of restoration, Jacob Boehme, she has been *gradually* stripped of even the residue of the wealth of her spiritual ornaments. She has been made to enter her own self-imposed Babylon captivity, with the gold and treasures taken away from the most unfaithful wife, and stashed away as a resource for those who have long cherished it. This state of spiritual *ichabod* is why scholarly bystanders, as well as many European and American Buddhist writers, mockingly refer to the contemporary West as being in the Post-Christian Era.

Also, for the same reason, the Holy Spirit of Lord Jesus did not send a minister from one of the numerous Christian sects to introduce his servant to the *Perfection of Wisdom*. This is the same Sophia which the disciples of the Christ are encouraged to seek after in The Letter of James, and the Letters of the Apostle Paul to the Corinthians, Ephesians, and Colossians. Rather, he chose a person of no repute. He selected a pure-hearted twenty-year-old servant to fellowship in Lord Jesus's name. This was arranged so that this sinner saved by grace, might behold the majesty of God in the face of Christ, viz., to recognize his own true face [*kensho* -JP.], or Christ nature in his mind essence.

However, to recognize the luminously cognizant and empty essence of one's own mind in the *face of Lord Jesus* is one thing, but to become stable in that recognition, beyond conceptual thought by means of the Inspeaking Practice [*Dzogchen* TIB.], is quite another. And it is a fiery crucible of afterwards searching high and low, throughout the many variable sects of Christianity, without ever having an introduction to the View validated, or receiving teachings on how to practice and mature what one has received. For divine Sophia [*Prajna-paramita* SKT.], the ultimate nature of Christ in us, is even the very luminous Body of Lord Jesus, his bride. *She is the one, which he brought with him in his Incarnation, through whom, and by his own shed blood, he has formed his Virgin ecclesia on planet Earth.*

Therefore, these poetic selections serve as an introductory meditational way bread. For it has been penned primarily for those seekers, who have prayed to know that wisdom coming down from above, and subsequent Christ-breathed anointing in order to receive her. As such, this text is also a reorienting compass, a true Polaris; it is ostensibly written for Christians who have exited onto any of multifarious well-beaten dead-end paths, into which reason void of faith in Jesus's name invariably leads. As such, the arrangement has been set within the framework of the nature of our human spirit, the human soul and their original *unified androgenous body*, the latter being lost in Adam's deep sleep.

Thou half-dead angel
Hear me!
I am as thou art—
Think not
that I have climbed up aloft
into Heaven
or behold with these eyes of flesh
Infinity—
Oh no!
I am a sinful— mortal man as thou art
must every day

grapple—struggle—fight
the Devil who afflicts
my corrupted nature—

————-

Yet, know this—
There is an eternal wrestling,
working and friendly
amiable rising up of *Love*
in which holy angels cannot enough rejoice—
most lovely sport therein—
Nor sufficiently enough sing
that beautiful
Te Deum Laudamus
of which I must here unfold to thee,
yet only by pieces
that thou mayst understand—

The first section, entitled "Lily," is viewed as when the spirit-soul is immersed into the divine *Lubet,* or first aspect of the *Mysterium Magnum* [L., *Ha Rakiya* HEB.], in which the seeker is born again. Concomitant with this act of desirous faith is the Holy Spirit's working, or stirring in the human will to bring about that *Feuerblitz* [G.], or *Flagrat* [L.]. This sanctifies the soul unto the salvation of Jesus the Christ in the *fifth, sixth, and seventh forms of the Gates of Paradise* [Nirvana Skt.]. The former is the divine reflex, or confession by faith in the most holy power of the Name Jesus, through grace stirring the insightful depths of Adonai's expansive opening [*Sherab* TIB.].

Next, the second section, "Lily-Rose," portrays sufficient grace. This is that of which Paul the Apostle speaks, whereby the spirit and soul participate in bearing the cross of the Lord Jesus's own suffering, even as a sword continuously piercing one's heart. This is that "cross-birth" of which the Theologian of Fire teaches, a dying to the world spirit [*Spiritus Mundi* L.], and living unto *God is Love*. Here, the will-spirit of the soul comes to experience the multi-layered veil of the *turba,* or disturbance of the five senses and sensate mind, which must be rent. For the latter is the dark obscurant, lying between its spirit-betrothal or espousal, and that divine marriage supper of the Lamb of God. Now, we behold in this the Christian parallel of *The Heart Sutra's* passage from *para gate's* partial enlightenment into the *parasangate bodhi svaha* of complete enlightenment.

Therefore, this present poetic work is designed with those seekers in mind, who dwell in the *state of illumination*; many are on the cusp of passing into the bridal unity of peace, that is, *the Perfection of Wisdom* [*Prajnaparamita* SKT.], or complete enlightenment. And needless to say, while in the body of our corrupted flesh, the latter state can *never be* without at least some subtle forms of conceptual missing the mark [sin -*hamartia* Gr.]. Yet, these only temporarily rest on the surface of the vast natural mind of Christ; they just come and go, being burned away by our awareness of emptiness and cognizance. For no person, due to the gross body of flesh, is without sin. However, we are openly commanded to be *holy and perfect in our will-spirit, even as our heavenly Father, who is Spirit, is holy in his perfect will.*

And the third section, "Pearl," is of a transfigurative nature, which mirrors the mercy of God's love [*Barmhertzigkeit* G.], working in the hearts of those who walk by simple faith. As such, many of these poems sing not only of the second aspect of that *Mysterium Magnum*, which lies hidden in our spirit's innermost center as the Image of God, but also, of our planet Earth in its paradisical or *Light-World* state [*Paradeisos* -Gr. *Dharmata* SKT.]. This *Light-World* is of the first and seventh forms, or eternal nature spirits, as One, realized in those who have been anointed with the perfect gift of Wisdom [*Sophia* Gr.]coming down from above. And as such, these children of the Father, both not only bear, but have widely-awakened to this their all things made new *Yield-Light Eco-System.* This is the virgin body of Christ in the eternal now, fulfilling the whole Earth and its atmospheres with splendor (glory) radiating from firmamental majesty. (Isa. 6:1). The poem "Jupiter, Sparkling Springing Up" is one example of this interfacing of the pristine upper waters above the *Rakiya* [HEB] with the corrupted waters below it (cf. Gen. 1:6).

Also, this section contains the seven poems directly associated with the *familiarity* or *Inspeaking practice*. They sing of how the Christian, who has been introduced to her or his own mind essence in the face of Lord Jesus, can go about bringing to completeness that once only received gift of grace. But please note, that these verses are not able of themselves to show that correct practice. Rather, their purpose is to enkindle your mind essence, that you may long for that practicum on how to bring your *glance* [*kensho* JP.]. or partially enlightened spirit, to complete fruition. However, as mentioned, extremely rare, precious and *openly hidden* are both the illuminated Christian texts, and the teachers of them, who are able to directly instruct the faithful seeker, hands-on, how to practice.

For with regard to the teachings themselves, you may have your book shelves packed with all the texts from the Anti-Nicaean Fathers, all the way up to Augustine of Hippo. From there, you may have garnered every Post-Nicaean teaching, dividing themselves up further through the Eastern and Western Churches. And from then on, you might know by heart the well-known mystics of them both, whether a St. Maximos the Confessor, a Theophan the Recluse, a St. John of the Cross, a Meister Eckhart, a Watchman Nee, or a Thomas Merton. However, not even one of these teachings, or all them crystallized, will ever be able to *directly* guide you, teaching your soul and spirit how to enter into a direct knowing of the light of God's splendor in the face of Jesus, *as your own true face*. For most of the teachings of the Church Fathers, and many of the church mystical teachings, like the *Philokalia*, have been laced with the subtly enervating poison of stoic and neo-platonic philosophies.

And the same pertains to the Buddhist Canon. You may know it all by heart, both the *Tripitaka* and the Tibetan Canon, but not one leaf of it will explain *directly* the nature of receiving a pointing out of the View, viz., your mind's essence [*tincture* -Rigpa TIB.], or its, so vital, subsequent recognition practice.

Dear Reader, there is in these days a high premium placed on Dzogchen texts (and the true teachers of them), beginning with

Garab Dorje's *Three Statements.* But within the Christian literary milieu, as mentioned above, the very first are contained in Jacob Boehme's *Way to Christ* collection, beginning with the tractate "The Supersensual Life." Next is *The Gates of the Paradisical Garden of Roses* from the tractate "Of True Repentance." The former is a direct instruction on the nature of the practice, but remains diffuse enough to keep a seeker after the Inspeaking Practice in doubt as to how exactly to apply it. Then the latter tractate, so affective and intimate in its mystical betrothal/marriage imagery, again, lies on the cusp of all but explaining the *nonmeditation* method of its daily practice. For the theologian's ever-present exhortation to "stand still and turn" finds our soul on the verge. Yet, we might be left without being given an explicit reminder of *just how to* stand still, and *who exactly is* this mysterious noble bride, called Sophia by *all the Greek texts of the Bible,* whose face our soul is encouraged to turn toward, and to look into.

Even the woman or man, who has been anointed from above in the mystical betrothal of the soul with Lord Jesus, still may not comprehend that this Sophia is the same one to whom *in Mary in the New Covenant of Grace,* he was partially united to as his pure bride, or wife of his youth. For the dark veil, hiding her exquisite face, has only once for the soul been lifted *in the glance.* In this sense, it is here noteworthy that Christianity's primary leitmotif for enlightenment, or being holy (*kadosh* HEB.) even as our Father is holy, is *the Marriage Supper of the Lamb.* This highly affective, and not mere symbolic, relationship to the Lord Christ, is an aspect that is missing in Dzogchen Buddhism, which tends toward a more cerebral approach. We see in the latter, rather the union of Samantabhadra (masculine) and Samantabhadri (feminine), the yab-yum, likened to a young man and woman meeting in secret tantric analogy. And because of this nuanced contrast between the two, chuppah songs are joyfully sprinkled here and there, as an aromatic seasoning, throughout parts of *Jacob Boehme's Songs.*

However, with the above in mind, among those Christians worshipping in the numerous denominations and persuasions, who have asked for and received this perfect wisdom-and-love

[*Barmhertzigkeit* G.], as in-breathed from above, rare it is to have ever even heard of Jacob Boehme. Neither have such seekers been taught how to *Inspeak*, viz., either mature *the View by recognition practice* within their own souls, or how to express it with their spirits to edify the church in faith.

Therefore, as mentioned above, the souls who have asked for, and received of the Holy Spirit, but have never been validated by their churches *in that noble Wisdom*, remain in a life-long crucible of quietly seeking desperation. Nevertheless, Jeanne-Marie Guyon's anointed book, *A Short and Easy Method of Prayer*, directly addresses the gaping lacuna in the wisdom practice within all the churches throughout the world. And for penning it, the author, to the end a faithful member of the Church in Rome, by the instigation of Louis the XIV's mistress and leading church prelates, was defamed, and then incarcerated for over ten years in the Bastille and other prisons.

Yet even today because of the anointing that lies upon its words to *directly guide* the reader, who has received that gift of wisdom-and-love in a recognition-*Inspeaking* practice, Guyon's noble book continues to be published. For it does what other spiritual tractates do not do. It is a hands-on practice guide to the soul on how it can, by the grace and mercy of the Lord Jesus, enter into a complete and holistic enlightenment. This, Guyon calls a being united with *God Alone*. As well, there is an excellent 1975 revision of the text, entitled *Experiencing the Depths of Jesus Christ*. This rendition restores the nuances of the French original, even as an art masterwork might have had layers of varnish removed.

Finally, as to the last section, "Jewel," *Jacob Boehme's Songs* touches the soul on the shoulder, and beckons her to look further beyond. The reader is encouraged to go past those contemporary claimants to be *the* interpreters of the Theologian of Fire. These are those deceivers who are often quite clueless, and groping in blindness, continue to take bits of his teachings out of context, and then torque these bits and pieces into grotesque shapes. Such detrital super-additions on the one side, along with so-called "scholarly" editions on the other, utterly miss the mark of Boehme's orthodox

Christian doctrine, and its penetrating awareness into the secrets of the one Faith.

Therefore, let us, as those children through whom wisdom can be justified, be watchful. With an acute peripheral vision, let our true minds be wary of those soul-devouring Scylla-like contemporary intellectual desecrators of Boehme's teachings. For they are ever collectors of information, but never penetrate into the knowledge of eternal truth. On the other hand, let those lovers of the *sweet Name Jesus* steer clear of the spirit-darkening Charybdis-like vortex, viz., that chaotic mish-mash of neo-Gnosticism, Paganism, Hermeticism, the Occult, neo-pseudo-theosophy and New Age faux-sciences. These, and their innumerable spawns, like cheap boot-legged whiskey, would twist the theologian's pure words according to their *ignis fatui*, the result being the deadening of the soul's mind essence. For in both the former and the latter, the one fraudulent purpose is ever to drive a dark wedge into the reader's mind essence, separating the *unity* of the precious setting of *the sacred Name Jesus* and the gem stone of Boehme's pure Christian theology.

Again, because of these things, the seeker after enlightenment should, as a simple child rebirthed of God in our Lord Christ's love, be even as a wary Odysseus. He or she should look askance at the neon online signs touting the name, "Jacob Boehme," whether they be societies, libraries, associations, online sites, universities, or so-called scholarly talks and lectures. For ninety percent of these are as scammers, who lift out only one tiny piece of a 1000-piece jigsaw puzzle. And rather than applying it to the compleat and holistic oeconomia of Boehme's Christian teachings, they take that tiny piece, and transmogrify it to their and their disciples' perdition, even as others did, and still do, to the pure Gospel doctrines of Paul the Apostle. Therefore, let us steer our precious human vessel strait down the true passage, or as the theologian phrases it, walk with him over this *very narrow bridge*.

With these weighty considerations in mind, we round off with a living parable that occurred in the Winter of 1985 at the annual Dallas International Gem and Jewelry Show. A master jeweler was one among thousands to attend the five-day event. After just a short while, the jeweler came to a particular booth, where the vendors had placed varying semi-precious and precious cut stones on a display table to sale. At first, nothing caught his attention.

Then as the master jeweler's eyes just cursorily passed over the stones, he noted that one of the gems seemed to catch the light differently than the others around it. He immediately bought it for two-hundred dollars, then hurried out of the auditorium into the Texas winter sunlight. His heart filled with great rejoicing as he lifted the gem up between his fingers. And before his eyes an extremely rare natural alexandrite shone brightly. Early the next morning, he telephoned the two local Dallas newspapers to report the details of his great good fortune. Articles were printed, with a protest not long in coming from the merchants of the stone, but to no avail. And the master jeweler would not resale this one-of-a-kind gem, but gave it to his wife as an anniversary gift.

The Holy Love-Spirit is as the master jeweler. He has gone in search for a highly precious stone, which for four-hundred years has been discarded by the church in the world as of no value. But dear reader, come and see what this shoe maker/glove merchant enigma is actually all about. It has been given to that lowly man to intimately know the eternal birth of *God the Heart-Son* in the Father's mind of eternal wisdom-and-love for the church.

For, here in this *Ungrund* [G.] is the priceless gem of the knowledge of God's eternal birth in humankind, that is, of the Noble Sophia. And the soul which wills to remain in that wisdom, emerging from God's love, is *born from above*. This is the *compleat* theology. Through this, the Holy Trinity has given its own essence to the spirit of our soul by the bodily Incarnation, Passion, Death on the Cross, and bodily Resurrection from the dead of Lord Jesus of Nazareth, the Messiah. He is the same who is eternally begotten, not made, one in being with God, the tenderly-loving Father.

And yet the Morning Star still sits waiting on the horizon. It is waiting for the recognition of these teachings from the Bride of the Lamb, which the *ecclesia disparate* has relegated to the back waters. Consequently, the true Aurora, or *Rising Dawn of the complete oeconomia of Adonai Sabaoth* for the church in the world is still, until now, being held back.

Therefore, *Jacob Boehme's Songs* is a seed from the element of the Heart of God, prophesied at the hands of holy angels, and now offered as a gift to your mind essence. It comes to you as a lighted taper, held before the looking glass of your soul's true face, for your perusal, inspiration, pure joy. For at this requisite 400 years, such a paschal candle is lighted for the last glimmerings before the dawn. This dawn is as the fragrant rose garden, in which the true Christian cosmogony for the 3rd Millenium church blossoms. And this small volume provides, until the shadows flee away, brief glimpses into those *Perfection of Wisdom* teachings, viz., the *Barmhertzigkeit* of the Anointed One's love for his bride.

> Lovely Candle
> Humble lovely mirth in meek Joy—
> No more anguish rising and burning—
> Only this delightful habitation divine—
> Only this *illustrate Majesty*
> shining bright, casting pleasant light—
> When the wick of the candle burns,
> no more pain and no woe,
> only a cause of the *glance of life*—
> There is no fire like the divine fire
> now flaming— now filled with God's Love—
> Of *the End* of all things
> sing my soul sublime
> of nature back to *The Beginning* turning—
> Lovely, this song of mirth in meek Joy—

The Firm Articles of the Christian Faith

BELOVED MIND, WE WRITE no conceits and tales; it is in earnest, as it is as much as our bodies and souls are worth. We must give a strict account of it, as being the talent that is committed to us. If any will be scandalized , viz., offended, at it, let them take heed what they do. Truly it is high time to wake up from sleep, for the Bridegroom comes.

We Christians believe and acknowledge that the eternal Word of God the Father became a true self-subsisting man (with body and soul) in the body, or womb, of the Virgin Mary, without Man's interposing, or having anything to do in it. For we believe that he was conceived by the Holy Spirit, and born of the body of the Virgin, without blemishing or defiling of her virgin purity or chastity.

Also, we believe, that in his human body he died and was buried.

Also, we believe that he descended into Hell, and has broken the bands of the Devil, wherewith he held Man captive in pieces, and redeemed the soul of Man.

Also, we believe, that he willingly died for our iniquities, and reconciling us to his Father. Therefore, he has brought us into favor (or grace) with him.

Also, we believe that he rose again from the dead on the third day, and ascended into Heaven, and there sits at the Right Hand of God.

Also, we believe that he shall come again at the Last Day, to judge the living and the dead, and take his bride to him, and condemn the ungodly.

Also, we believe that he has a Christian Church here upon Earth, which is begotten in his blood and death. And it is made so one Body with many members, which he cherishes, and governs with his Holy Spirit and Word. Again, he unites it continually by the holy Baptism of his own appointing, and by the sacrament of his Body and Blood to one only Body in himself.

Also, we believe that he protects and defends the same, and keeps it in one mind.

TP 17.115-6

Poetic Prologue

A SUDDEN SHOWER

My children of the soul's *magia* divine
I am just the hand penning these mysteries sublime
as the true starred Hand of God stirs up his own,
so think not of the lover of *Wisdom's* jeweled stone
or the beauty of her luminosities as from me,
since nothing here you may read my own work be;
for I have broken my will and shall write nothing
but by the direction of God's *Love-Spirit* hastening,
that burning *Fire* often forcing forward speedily,
after it this hand and pen dashing directly,
it coming and then going as *a sudden shower*,
hitting whatever it lights upon with power—
If it were possible to comprehend and write all told
which my mind in the *Divine Chaos* beholds,
far deeper the ground, and three times more,
as an eternal remembrance for the defect restored—

Lily

A GOOD FRIDAY, FALLING

Love has God's Eyes—
When the rain drops
leave their mother Eave
letting go—
only
pure Virgin thoughts—

MY FIRST MOTHER

I had to die again
to go back into my *First Mother*
chosen again to be her Child
to stand again in the *Verbum Fiat*
of the *expressed Word*
to enter once more into *that* which I was
in the Beginning
before I was born
before I was conceived—
And there *it was good*—
for I stood again in that *Root*
one with the only Will of Eternity
from whence I came forth,
your *beginnings* of all things
only and barely a *desire*—
No-thing but pregnant *with magic,*
your eternal *Voice* of joy-figurized
in my looking-glass to behold
indestructible fixities—
Souls of men watching angels,
expressions of eternities into *time,*
wonders of my Lord's *good* pleasure,
my only *Mother's* possibilities,
seed-bearing of timeless Wisdom—
my *Sophia*—

THE WIND

Like a Nor'easter
swift Leviathan flees
before the *Quiet Chaos*,
of your *One breathing*
coming and going
as You please,
no one knowing
where, but see there
a thunder-clap's enkindled
ethereal blaze
goes before—
A stroke in the cold
enfolding into hail,
but congealing into drops
at the light's desire—
Meekness changing ice
into mere mist
distilling upon the Earth—
Come—
Open the chamber window—
A cool breeze follows
whirling—
Listen—
Can you hear the *Voice*?
Nature's forms awakening
a turning Wheel of

this threefold breathing
carrying their Spirit
The Wind—

38

THE RUBIED CICADA

Rubied cicada, this Louisiana night begrace,
cithara it hid beneath your fragile caramel shell,
clinging to the great oak with its gray Spanish lace—
Fiery orb of the heart's first cardiac pulse
on the twentieth day, enter the clinging embryo—
kindling of the child's *spirit*, springing impulse
life of our light at the blood's first flow,
you are God's fiery breath, man's deep urge to know all—
an eye in the eternal abyss to convey
your fabric, nature's *seven fountains'* bestowal,
seed begotten of the divine essential rays—
immortal soul, God-created to conceive his ways,
as our eternal *archaeus* in this fragile body dwells,
our house and instrument till we leave this place—

MY DEAR VIRGIN

When our soul is drawn
through *the Deep Gate*
of the Father's *tender love,*
it sees Lord Jesus and sings—
This is my Virgin
whom I lost in Adam
when she was changed
into an earthly woman—
Now I have found again
my dear Virgin
who sprang from my body—
I will no more let her go—
She is mine,
my flesh and blood,
my strength and power
whom I lost in Adam—
Her I will retain—
Friendly Beauty
chaste fruit
power and virtue—
Oh, a friendly retaining!

HOT LOVE OIL

When God's *Heart-Son* held your love-seed in his Hand
the hour the Fell One set the world on fire,
against the Father his legions raged, made their stand,
burning the World's fabric into cold wrath dire,
God's pure *salniter* turning a seething mire,
but held back by the *Word* from becoming black Earth,
and your *drop of life's essence* from the pyre—
Then the hidden Heart's starred right Hand held your soul's birth,
God's Son glancing with his hot love upon your worth—

So, your oil, sacred fiery love-drop of Heaven
rose from the glowing waters through such *sude's* might
whiter than anything in nature, God's leaven
impregnated with a young son, reaching the Light
catching hold of the Son of Man's fiery sight
conceived in Christ before the world's foundation,
before He came unto his own in this world's night,
embracing till the *Sixth Day* of the drop's fountains—
Seven eternal spirits—*Man's living soul* in creation—

WHAT GRACE IS THIS?

What Grace is this?
Baptized, O Virgin Mother
in the font of your sweet *Voice,*
while still a fat crawling baby
lifted above the bitter ground
of disparately tinctured parents
of fighting fire and water—
the fire of this soul,
the water life of this spirit;
Mars and *Venus*
struggling *in utero*
seed of an ill-begotten bed,
this hardened heart their heir,
deadened ground, mine own will
bound *in time* beyond repair—
Yet
What grace is this?
Your Right Hand fashioning these parts
even in my mother's womb—
Jesus weeping—
sweet Mercy's choice,
greater than sin, *Hell* and death
calling
"Come forth from your tomb of flesh!"
O Virgin-Son of Man's *Voice*—
Most Holy Sweet Power,

LILY

Seed of the heavenly virginity
birthing this chosen man-child
out unto your abyssal Self—
Restored
holy Temple of God—

HERTZ IS THE FLASH: *FEUERBLITZ* I

Christ, *you* break the seven seals in Man's soul—
Flash of Lightning captivate the four forms,
for in the cloud you have set your *Rainbow*
giving love and joy after harsh storms—
Once bound up in the matrix of the wrath,
none of these seven seals able to be broke open
by no one in Heaven nor in the Crystal Bath—
Yet our Champion, the *Feuerblitz* has spoken—
Voice of God's power raising bodies dead—
Flagrat in the Temple rending the Veil
manifest the clear face of God instead—
Sharpened Eternity harrowing Hell—
Hertz—release of the daughter of my tongue,
White Rose of our Resurrection, this my song—

LOVELY, GENTLE, AND STILL

Dive into Love's delightful birth
gentle, lovely and still,
terror to that anxiety—
that hidden hollowness called Hell—
Father, yourself, so tenderly loving,
You give birth to my Mother,
Virgin Wisdom temper mild—
This soul's thirst after freedom,
Love-fire's longing fulfilled,
the Heart-Son's only Child
of wondrous awe-filled Chaos
awaiting the water's breaking—
Breathings of these silent reflections
of your eternal unfathomable will,
so lovely, gentle, and still—

HE SHOOTS UP AS A LILY

Reason, if of thy past fame but a spark
of our native land from which we've gone out,
how would thou long for it, lost in the dark—
How wouldst thou toss this wicked Devil out!
O most worthy Light bring us back again—
We now with Adam are fallen asleep,
Our long dream in the demon's net amend—
Our salvation, let us once again see—
Come then, *Champion Breaker Through* of death—
Hero crush this corrupted kingdom of Earth!
A cordial from Zion give to refresh
this return to our true native land, Thy rebirth—
Lo, all hills and vales are full of His glory—
Hallelujah! He shoots up as a Lily—

SPARK

Faith's humble spark, once held back and hindered
with merely a fiery dark desire
burns in anguish, in despair's horror,
possessing no seed — no hope to aspire,
but just three essential fountains of malignity—
There no awe-filled diving— no sinking down
when your soul is void of meeknesssomighty—
no plumbing calm depths through death to be found—
Now humble spark pierce these five brimstones bitter,
sunder this giddy maelstrom, *wrath's* wheel,
hard heart of the soul, this circle of fire,
and sink down through death to the *divine Light-World*—
this door of the *Deep* between Heaven and Hell—
Here a twig buds, all your soul's bane to quell—

SURRENDER, FALLING

Behold these pearls to impart,
More and more to you falling,
disclosed in this glad employ—
Discovery in your seeking trust
affording me this special joy
to recreate myself thus
with you in God's Heart—

Entirely like you Man is made—
Spirit, my God, Light-flaming holy—
But in yourself only— nothing is like you
save ungrounded Splendor—nothing grasped—
No spirit, being or tinctured hue,
but an *eternal stillness* only,
except our spirit be formed in *Love-Fire's* pervade—

Now behold this sinking down like dying,
our fiery source giving itself o'er,
falling, freely surrendering
out of harm's way, nothing hindering
into that freedom piercing all pain
immersed into the impassible evermore,
descending even deeper now undying—

Deliver us from the torment of fiery anguish—
keeping fire's sharpness in free *lubet's* allay,

freedom receiving the *Flagrat* to become our desire,

from the painful source sinking down, turn into *Tincture*—

Our soul's drawing into Joy— freedom's rejoicing choir

passing out of self-will into life's exceeding rapture,

to express which only an angelic tongue could say—

FLEE NAKEDLY

Young Man
in linen limned—
Your little light's
distancing deceit
Go out of your mind—
tear through
into sheer *Mercy*—
Break off—
Go forth from your *Will*
from all your thoughts,
leaving all behind
in grasping hands
Life's pride & anguish
envy and terror—
torches, lanterns, weapons—
No helper to appear
for fear in the night—
Now depart—
flee nakedly
if your *spirit's will*
would follow *Me*—
Experience full well
this sparkle of
Love's agony—
Love's healing travail
and only remedy

leading *Me* away—
This dust of fierce death
breaking down
in judgement's peace
turning round—
Yourself now only
a naked spirit
sinking down—
Wings of a dove—flee
into *faith's* bright night—
Look! My hands, my feet—
Sparkling *White Clear Light*—
Put on God's Love—

FRUITFUL RAIN IN YOUR STILL MOTHER

May you be found worthy to hear the Voice
of the noble Bridegroom who calls his bride to rejoice,
to bring her home in this very lovely Gate—
This your hungry spirit-soul, so weary, so faint,
desirous of the still meekness and rest
would go forth from the Driver's power to molest
to satiate itself in the meek-and-still domain
thereby Christ's heavenly body to sustain—
Born of this calm humility— my beloved mind
in the Wisdom of God before this world's *time*
of the Love of God in the *Eternal Virgin*—
In your still eternal Mother, a fruitful rain—

But how are you in such unquietness so great—
endless hunger and thirst after food to abate?
O that the time of refreshment were come!
For this poor soul 'neath wishing and panting succumbs—
After its lonely evening, a day's morning cries,
and the night longs after the day's bright Eye—
There is no place nor rest from the Driver—
on and on till it finds the bosom of its *Mother*,
as one escaped great battle where one lays down,
who dare not lift up his head for fear of being found,
so our soul sticks in such great unquietness
as it is with a soldier in a fight's duress—
continually in expectation of death

where enemies on every side upon him press—
Or as one fallen into a deep sea
and sees no shore, swimming there dangerously
where the water into his mouth e'er goes,
who sighs and desires Heaven's help to bestow—
Or like one who is into a deep pit falling,
who expects help from above and keeps calling—
Our soul searching its flesh, blood and bones, too, remiss,
its own enemies leading it into the abyss—
this *Spiritus Mundi* draws it—bows it down to the ground
and in the deep-water desires it to drown—
Also, the Devil would fain throw it into Hell
with no helper about, all torments to quell,

till it raise itself, God's *Love* and *Mercy* take,
all whatsoever is in its house to forsake,
going forth from all its thoughts in its own will
into the Mercy of God, its mind now still,
into our *first Mother* where it was a pure seed
before the creation of this world, that meed—
And when it comes here, the same Word it finds,
which created it is become a *Man Divine*
of our humanity—so cast yourself down, eat
of his pure and new *Virgin Body* replete
in which there is no source of enmity,
but only a mere desirous loving meekly—
the Holy Spirit leading our soul out of prison
for it to eat at Christ's banqueting provision—
sitting among the children of the Father's love,
how humbled it is that the Holy Ghost, the Dove
has delivered it from the strife of the battle wild—

Then God has a true, obedient and meek child—
The soul pressing forth out of this sea of misery
resting in the Father's bosom of maternity—

CARMEL PACIFIC *GELASSENHEIT*, MARCH, 1973

As the gracious, amiable, joyful light so blessed
of God's Son shines its beam into loving Angels' hearts
all their bodily powers kindled—a joyful *love fire* to impart—
Singing—ringing forth praises neither I nor creature can express
with this song may the Reader into *eternal life* be drawn
when the gracious, blessed, and joyful glance so amiable
such that I am unable to write down, my hand so trembles,
as the sweet Son of God's power shines into the whole Father's dawn!
His shaved head bobbed like a buoy above the Pacific calm
as my Soul stood stranded on the white Carmel sand—
Then his arm and hand lifted, beckoning as though I'd understand
to come out, be drawn into the fearless Deep's healing balm—
But struggle as the holy patriarch, Jacob, did you must—
Wrestling the Holy One of Israel the night's long course
till the dawning of the Day, and morning redness breaks forth
never to give over until God does bless, his Word your trust—
the Holy Spirit birthing his *love fire* form in thee
kindled by the gracious—blessed—lovely light and power sweet
holding on in your earnestness, allowing for no defeat,
then will his fire come suddenly—like lightening decreed—
Experiencing this, quite another man you will become
like *the Salt Doll measuring God's Deep*, now a homecoming Son—

SHOOTING FORTH BRIGHT INTO THE FAIR LILY

Child of God, best kernel of nature
who would fain live, balm in the Good,
travail in desire's birth of the holy life—
Bud forth out of the bestial image,
out of mixed bad and good be *born again*
out of the wild animal impulse—fell earthly feature
to the noble *Image of God* be reborn in Light
shooting forth bright into the fair Lily—
Bud, sprout, grow and be strengthened in God's form,
letting your essences blossom, bear fruit
flourishing in Christ Jesus, our fair Tree of Paradise—

Now we wish to impart to our twigs
and fellow noble branches in our sacred Tree
in which we all have being and grow—
Our sap, savor and blessed essence,
so that we may rejoice one with another
and urge all *Children* to ponder
that each bough and twig help to shelter
the other from the storm—
And, so we commend ourselves to your love—

DESCENT INTO THE *RAKIYA*

Are not You the One who fills all things to sate,
not just some heaven afar off above *the situate*?
Here! Now! Your *firmament* pure expanse liquified
e'en as the out-spoken Wisdom's rich milk clarified—
your endless Gulf 'tween time and *eterne* to bestow,
morning's womb bearing waters above and below
as we sink down awe-struck, immersed in such churning grace,
your *spirating* Holy Love Spirit's hushed motion to embrace
this baptism's soul-magnifying liquid the real healing ground,
now *solidified* in the Spirit's seed-bearing sound—

Great secret of the Expressed Word in which our God's
Trinity is revealed—Bless now this fellowship's laud,
as we sink not to any nadir, but to your clear Center—
Dear wonder mild— our *Immanuel* by stirring tender—
Taste and see, my soul, how sweet this no-substance known,
of what such *sounding spiritual* Word's speaking forth is
in our descent past the sharks of sharp wrathfulness,
where no colours are known in this mysterious *Abysm*,
where they lie hidden in Its overflowing healing chrism—
Then how pleasant a pouring forth in sweet-breathing grace
when this *glance of Majesty* lets us behold your face—

BLADE

Blade cut away this I again—
Tincture deep into darkness—
Bare these five bitter senses—
Once more the cold hard gristle
of my unbroken will's tempest,
this diminishing *Self* harrow—
My *Yes* willingly receiving
Delight's magical motions deft—
Her Light-honed edges
slicing away this bitter sound—
Blade down breathing e'en
past faith & hope's austere desire
down to sweet white marrow
to love-on-fire holy
into Joy's three deepest
Somethingless Beauties—

DELIGHT DRAW ME

Out of *Your* still Nothing
Delight draw me—
Pass through with
these sweet breathings
of desire's stirring grace,
this *place prepared*
for our *Good* pleasure,
Love's highest ground
in your wondrous Will awestruck
to be here only
in this pregnant *magic*—
This birthplace beyond self
where I found *You*—
God begetting God:
my Father & my Heart—
From both
the Holy *Love-Spirit's* procession
drawing deeper in—
O Effectual Sensibility!
This motion of knowing
Who *You* are
and who I am
in this *Love-Taste*—
this Root and Ground of eternal life—
Delight draw me—
Breathe forth your *Inspirating*

to here plant,
conceive the only *Holy Son*
Anointing
my spirit's barren womb—
This *Seed*
the Eternal One—

OUT OF THE HEART OF DARKNESS

Will-Spirit
burning in sparkling *Infinity*
who would be free
longing to conceive again
to be born again
at the breaking of the dark waters
Out of captive torment—
Out of the heart of darkness—
These four torture chambers
of the whole world
being on fire—
Noble mind
full of anguish
of this world's afflictions,
arise with that
other conceived Will—
The smell and virtue,
Essences of the *Lily*
springing up in wonders—
Enter into your *true self*
as sudden lightning—
Living Flame
take hold of this *other World*
where the *Gate of Heaven*
stands wide open,
the Bride intreating:

Come
Drink and taste
pure wonder—
Desire God's light—
Be our Noble Image,
once extinguished
now born out of death—
Death of the heart's
dying poison
kindling this white and clear
Sparkling Fire of Life
as we come into
the *Virgin's embrace*—

Lily-Rose

BLOSSOM IN THE TIME OF THE LILY-ROSE

Open Fountain of God springing up in the *Heart-Son*—
Lord Christ be our refreshment and *Light-Constant*—
And for your heart's delight, I wish you true knowledge divine
from these writings where many a noble rosebud awaits—
Heaven's vouchsafe from your soul's center to unfold
when the *Lily-Rose* blossoms in sweet smelling purity
as a paradisical lily-twig sublime loves
in Jesus' Rose-Garden to grow and bear fruit—
That streams out of his fountain from you might flow,
his *Child* weaned on the Spirit's open doors of wonders
finding all mysteries in the Father's *chaste Virgin mind*—

NIGHTS, ZION DOWNTOWN

Your *Flash Light* keeps me up nights
working in the dark on your love poems,
which *Minnesinger's* epic meter has no copyright—
Pure babes plucked from the fiery dust
of nigh forgotten tomes—
Like a distained *Denarius Dei* these diamond songs
trampled o'er by the passing intellectual throngs
of a sole stranger in his strange Fatherland banned,
yet each quiring leaf bears your watermark—
Illuminated Script of
golden strings plucked by my Lord's own *Hand,*
pure tinctured playing to which mere children hark—

Mocking and deriding what your mind cannot understand,
You scoff and say: What ails this foolish archaic clown?
When will he have done with his dreaming?
But when I speak and write it's not from myself,
rather from the Mother's knowing and seeing—
For I am dead and as a nothing,
and would willingly take my ease,
fly away to the wilderness and be at rest—
Yet, live I in cares, labour, fear and trembling's anguish—
For like other men, I am also clothed in Adam's skin,
and yet live also in the hope of Israel—
For that God who created the Cosmos is too strong for me,
when in the lightning tempest the depths of the future Mysteries

are shewn—
So sleep on in your fleshly lusts—
See what kind of dream this will be!

Your *Flash Light* keeps me up all night
harkening to the happy cry of the new-born
firstlings of our love's ungrounded flight
coming back to Earth cradled
beyond this world's bourne
of these wild nights ours to dance and sing
holding hands—whirling sweet wine—Sophia's rounds
never knowing what the sober sunshine brings
after wee hours love-wrestling in Zion Downtown—

ONCE WHEN I WAS YOURS

Kindle again my soul in that same essence
in which You once drew me into your
life-springing from *Wisdom's* eternal fount
out of my despair's miserable house
into your power of burning Love-desire
in Father's will, tender and immortal
magically through my longing's fiery birth canal
out of its pregnant Mother and into
such *burning white clear Light*—

Kindle like when my heart so felt and knew it,
becoming joyous laughter, so death-breaking
into pieces and budding forth,
so springing up into your *Light-World*—

Now I die—
Make my fire a *Love-Desire* again
in your thirsting after my poor *embondaged* soul—
You who came in Adam's place
bring *my darling* once more out of captive fierceness
into your heavenly healing flesh and blood,
and scatter this devouring darkness within—
Enkindle Luna's love-shining even now—
Such a gentle shower to rain down
that I once knew when I was yours—

THE WIDOW'S WALK

As a New Gloucester whaler's wife day and night looks out
from her widow's walk toward the Atlantic Deep,
so this instrument, my soul, peers into the Godhead's Depths,
waiting for the sounds— which strings the will's spirit touches—
Even to know this *Joy even as I am known,*
even as a golden harp played upon—its form understands
that furtherest from his Finger's touch, the rest is only silence
rousing my ear to deafness as He departs,
packing up with him all my *Jubilates*—
All these angel-like revelations, but only in part—
Then I know nothing—as strings that now only lie still,
but merely the elementary and earthly things of this world—
Nothing heard nor understood, but only a dumb essence—

YOU KNOW THIS LOVE WELL

Draw near and intimately know this yearning
of our soul for this love nonpareil—
When your life-spirit is joined with God, you know it well,
but your bestial body, *as if* lightened, gets only a glimpse,
as the soul's innermost birth through the outermost tears—
the Holy Ghost's bliss breaking through your *Gates of Hell*—
Yet too soon this *Joy* to your outer flesh folds up—shuts again,
for the wrath of God bolts up once more the *Three Heavens*—

As a woman with child is in her travail and fears
would fain bring forth her child, but to no avail,
so, this loving-light to your outward man is gone—
You now walk up and down in anxious birth, full of throes—
Such the bestial body, once it tastes the sweetness of God,
then it ever hungers and thirsts after this exquisite love,
as the Devil in wrath's power opposes—O painful woe
with nothing but battles and warring in your births—

Dear Reader, not for mine own glory, but for your comfort,
if you be minded to walk with me over this narrow bridge,
then be not suddenly discouraged, and distrustful
when the *Gates of Hell*, God's wrath meet you, their dearth—
So come with me o'er this narrow overpass of fleshy birth
to yon green meadow, where death's darkness does not reach,
there through all of our hurts sustained to rejoice and rule,
though at present the world does account us for fools—

EAGLE: *THE INSPOKEN UNGRUND*

Love has God's Eyes—
Beauty's perfection—
Mirrored plume-less pinions
everywhere an eye within
and without, all things *in your*
no motion besides the Spirit's
eternal first *Beginning*
and eternal first *End*—
Before this looking-glass
come and see
hovering with wings outstretched
your will-spirit soaring upon
something much better, much nobler—
Its own *still* groundless desire
circling, drawing in merely *your true Self*
Out of the forms of awakened fire—
Out of the mind's torture-chamber—
Out of death into the Right Life
beyond suffering's bane
dying in *the* Christ's death—
Rising in his *cross-birth*,
caught up again into
this ninth hour's *no-thingness*—
Come, too, and see
our Virgin's maternity
from consuming fiery heat

birthing us in this *Pure Element*
her warm Silent-*outspoken body*—
Our dying into freedom again—
O Soul, wait in silence for God alone,
O fledgling of eternity's aerie
upon his *Inspoken Ungrund* buoyed—
Our lifting up into luminous likeness—
See the wonders of *His Majesty*
higher than our lost horizons
searching *past thoughts seeking*
without striving, without enquiry—
Our only prey this playfulness—
Seeking and finding What it is—
Flight beyond being
yet reflection of all beings—
Eternity's lovely ecstasy,
Joy of all the Earth—

THE HINGE

Soul, essential fire in the eye of eternity,
perfect as a fiery globe standing in the center—
Wheel of *Natura's first four forms*—like God's paternity,
desirous of the consuming glimmering ember
or else the substance of *Love* in the *Light* to tender—
Your will drawn like a moth to the power of the fire
or your spirit's *Magia* towards the Heart-Son's splendour—
One figure only fiery—else love-light your attire,
as the life-spirit's will yearns, so the image it acquires—

If the will of the soul changes, its form will also change—
So out of your fiery self into Christ's Light *imaginate*,
as a flower buds from the earth, your fire-light exchange
like the Moon at the glance of the Sun doth radiate
and let your image stand in God's glorious weight
changed into meekness out of its fiery property—
Then be God's child in flowing light and fervent love sate,
Christ's virtues in living water's substantiality
as your essential fire desires only Majesty—

But if your soul *imaginates* into greed to partake,
its essential fire earthly figures desiring,
as envy and pride—those images the soul's *fiat* will make,
its *turba* destroying *the Form Divine* by imaging,
the galactic elemental power acquiring
into the inward *that* outward dimension's power brought,

the soul's fire becoming pregnant, and it retaining
a very difficult to be vanquished beastly shape wrought
devouring the Image of God in the deadly wrath—

So, it is not an easy matter to be a Christian
continually striving against flesh and blood's reasoning,
our will-spirit turned to mercy and love's divine admission,
earthly goods and pleasures not recognizing,
this *turba* to God's image, our lust's poisoning,
except the soul's will turn round and pierce into God's *Love*,
getting back *only in this life* that image worth obtaining—
For where your heart is, there also is your treasure trove,
the pure from the unclean severed on that Last Day thereof—

NO MERE ANGEL

Noli tangere!
No mere angel
standing in the ground
of the Promised Land
of the gentle Light's Despiser,
Place of this fire-Lord's
enkindled *Sulphur*—
Yet not quite dead,
longing to be delivered from Vanity
it looks to you
thou greater mystery than the angels,
those flames of fire
illustrate with light—

So let not the Liar strike fire
in the hard sour *Flash*,
this sounding of his hellish dwelling—
Der Geist ist willing—
So sweet to the taste
this Hell's proprium,
but bitter to the belly—
aber das Fleisch ist schwach—

So hark not
the sudden pealing thunder—
Aspire not your *Pearl* into phantasy
broken off from the *Unity*,

but stand fast in the evil day,
Thou no mere angel—
spirit interfacing matter,
flesh half-heavenly
and half-earthly,
sweet-smelling flower
but scion of the Earth
sprung from the sacred *Limbus*,
fair judicial blossom
of *prima materia* extract—
Now seal up the seven thunders
thou greatest mystery of God.
Inscribe them not on your heart—

MARRIED TO A BEAST

God created Adam in *Noble Sophia's* virginity,
Man's rose-garden of delight in himself fair,
surrendered in divine harmony—
Adam yet in God's Love, and the woman *in* him dear,
a Virgin in Wisdom and sweetness pure,
the heavenly life penetrating the earthly part,
all in equal measure and weight by divine art—

As time is in God, and God is in time,
the fruits of her delighting himself he ate,
extract of the *Sixth Day's* mystery divine
in the *matrix of Venus* his own love *satiate*—
Fiery tincture's great joyous *delection* to create,
he *both man and woman* in light's tinctured science,
ruling all creatures, standing in equal essence—

Then the serpentine subtly was manifest
by him who a lord o'er fire and light would have been
to extinguish the *Light*—despising all gentleness,
he was cast out in his erstwhile fire-lord's wishing
to dwell in darkness—the abyssal habitation,
off to corrupt Adam's precious *Image*—now forlorn,
Man passed into a fell state—God's form withdrawn—

Through him who rules in nature's corruption
the loving Man/Woman lost androgyny,

now beast of all beasts after the earthly extraction—
There are a great variety of animal properties—
a reptile, wolf, bear, dog, bull, lion all creaturely,
so, a cat, horse, cock, toad and snake all with feral features
as there are on the Earth, so many kinds of creatures—

Varied likewise is earthly Man's breeding,
all according to the potent starry influence,
making the seed's property in the time of the seeding,
fleshly desire brought forth in earthly confluence—
Yet not a brute shape in man's outward inheritance.
but in the earthly *Limus* the desirous figure,
so, man's body with such a beast must be beleaguered

driving him into the wild—winding him up,
not such in outward form, but really in earthly essence,
yet this beast in each puts forth its *Signature* corrupt—
Do but heed and well mind the same, and you may sense it—
Hence Christ called those Pharisees vipers and serpents,
other wicked he deemed ravening wolves or such,
for in their earthly essence they were as much–

For as the *Limbic Body* is, so the spirit's part
doth inwardly figure and form its measure—
Where then is our will and heart,
there also our image and treasure—
But the poor soul stands in this imprisoned terror
to such a beast married and bound,
unless that a man or woman be *new born*—

Forsake this feral property as dear children
or we can not possess the *Kingdom of Heaven,*
for which ground in the Old, God ordained circumcision,
a sign that this member will be removed in humans,
not appearing with them in *Eternity's mansions*—
So Christ had to take on him the form of a man,
though inwardly in *the Virgin Image* he did stand—

For we are to be baptized in Christ's Spirit in the New,
yet not worthy our iniquitous brute-like man,
but on *the Wild Earth at the Last Day* retains its due
to be consumed by the fiery Hand of God's fan—
So, the man's pure fire's property must command,
while the woman's light his flaming quality softens
bringing it into the mild *Image of God's blossom*—

STAND BEFORE THE CRIB WHERE JESUS IS BORN

My beloved seeking mind, I would
if I could, willing write it in your heart
to seek nothing else but the Heart of God, the Word
in the crib among the oxen in the stable dark
in the night if you find It, Christ to impart
together with the Father, Word and Holy Ghost,
eternal nature, Paradise and angels' vast part—
Then you will see your reason's lingering boast
reeling as a drunken man, to be very lost—

So no need to break your mind with thoughts high—
With high fancies and conceits you find no ground—
Only incline your mind to God's *Barmhertzigkeit,*
and be born out of God's Heart, the Word profound
in the Center of your life, his light to crown,
that you be *one* with him, the *Light* of your life
from Christ Jesus, Word in the Father, God's Son—
Bright glance and sweet power of eternity's Light
must be born in you, become Man, *God's delight*—

You are in the dark stable otherwise,
and go about feeling and groping,
looking for Christ, who's a great way off, you surmise,
at the right-hand of God opining
to seek Him among the stars your mind casting,

misrepresenting God—like the Sophists teach
as dwelling afar off, somewhere everlasting,
as the Devil above the Heart of God would reach,
yet remains still in eternal nature's dark breach—

With blind reason it also is,
seeking God in the darkness—sitting in the gloom,
but *all is full of God*—He shines in the darkness—
Find him everywhere, there to commune,
for God hidden in the dark heart, in your *Light-World blooms*—
It will be *opened unto you if you knock*
by the Holy Spirit, the key in the *Centrum*—
So in the desires of the flesh put no stock,
but let true *earnestI-Penny's Repentance* be your will's rock—

Now bring reason and musings into the Mercy of God
to be molded in you his *Beloved Heart* mild,
to stand by the crib where Jesus is born, awed—
Then incline yourself before the Child—
Christ born in you, pledging him your heart reconciled,
though oft times He is denied to you by the Devil—
Yet stand strong a light in the thorny center's trial,
now a sprout of God's splendour begirt with dark peril,
sprung of glooming nature, yet glory's Child nonpareil—

FEUERBLITZ II

Father, your love brings me here gainsaid—
I've entered into this strange world unknowing,
Death's death rising up at this my dismay—
Your flashing throne and pure love flowing,
these searing but soft torches my mort body enter
into this God-struggling hope in Christ—
Glimpse moving upon the Cross in the Center,
cutting that raven-black cloak hiding your face
in twain; This temple's veil your *Sunburst* rending—
Now *Name Jesus*— joyful lightning fork reveal,
sharpen my glance toward eternity's mending—
Hertz—these four supernal founts here unseal,
release my soul from *cold dark matter's* bondage—
In your *Word of Power, my true Body*'s homage—

KNOW THYSELF: *THE ENEMY WITHIN*

Turning to be as little children is your treasure,
not conscious of any falsehood or deceit's mistrust,
learning to know ourselves in highest measure,
for the Devil daily misleads and ensnares us
that we to our God and Father bear enmity—
Such a very unsafe pilgrimage to walk—
For within us we carry our worst enemy,
which we ourselves hide desiring to know it not,
our corrupt nature—the most horrid guest of all,
our earthly imagination—the torture chamber
marrying us to the Devil's lusting festival,
casting our soul headlong into God's anger—

Hence to know this enemy is for you most needful—
What he is, who he is and whence he is,
and how the Devil is allied with him so dreadful—
How they help one another for perdition to seize us,
to die and perish for our enemy's sake,
which dwells in us, and Man's very half if truth be told—
that is, a forgetting of all *Good* and to forsake
God and all his creatures as forever our foes—

For you are in both good and evil: Yourself learn to know,
and overcome in the promise of eternal life
as God's children living in his kingdom, Christ bestowed—
This evil ignorance and deceit—its spawned strife

cause the five bitter senses' anguished stinging
not to be subdued the more resisted it is
the more sting in Man's outward nature bringing—
An inimical bitter mind and envious
into which soul's thoughts the Devil winds himself sear,
your will burning—ne'er ending with envy's fiery darts,
never speaking any good, but vanity mere—
Producing liars, gossips, back bitters and false hearts,
this bitter, *compunctive* raging essence of pain
making in the Earth a strong harsh soul-distain—

But when the soul these earthly bestial thoughts reject
in meekness, holding the promise of eternity,
when on *the Last Day in a new Body* we resurrect,
burying in the earthly field our enemy,
all evil and pain our souls shall live above
with God in perfect Joy, loveliness and bliss—
So of God's desiring will seek meekness and love,
and to stand strong in what God's wrath and the Devil is,
but mostly to know how Man's soul is eternal,
for thus can we know God's *tender love* paternal—

BURNING COLD NIGHT

Burning cold night
in your radiant starry elements—
Oh how I wonder *how*
your protons and electrons
raging and raving plasmic sounds
of no Stradivari strings,
but violent discordant cat gut
are infecting this imagination
plunging my will-spirit deeper,
diving into the dark *Vorboten*—
Searching into this abyssal
whole world on fire—
Making me tremble,
making me burn *to be*
beyond Love's surrender
beyond Christ's Virgin Wisdom,
ever pushing higher, quicker, faster
only shaker-mover *Me*
up to the breast a *Cocytus* frozen,
alone master of my spirit's fate—
Only captain of my soul elevate,
deceitful kindled cold fire
just giving the power and virtue
of God's bright candle
the Snuff—

PREGNANT

I am pregnant—
Are you pregnant, too?
With November's night-shade
longed-after fruit
burning berries, honey-sweet
in the mind's mouth
but bitter stinging
in the will's belly,
our *imaginating an other*
our magical fire's
substantial desire
Seizing in love—
Seizing in wrath–
Images of earthly matter,
frail perishable root
this *something* in torment
corrupting our *no-thing's*
noble image of light with:
Ideas of the eye's object
of the ear's hearing
of the nose's smelling
of the tongue's tasting
of the body's touching
carrying *phantasies* into
our mind's thoughts
fevered with the fuel

of nature's burning
temporal, fierce and frail
our soul's pure fire
feeding upon tainted food—
foreign and feral these
things we crave after,
things our Self requires
for these delights yearning
that "I" might remain
pregnant . . . ever
preserved burning in
this twilight sickness dim—

FORKED LIGHTNING: *FEUERBLITZ* III

Fire flash, thou fourth form of this dark weald
where inward worlds, dark and light separate,
since thy will-spirit's choice plunges whither it will.
free to lay hold of, to master its fate—
Face the *Heart-Son's* gaze of eternity clear,
or as reason's cow mazed at a new stable gate—
One sinking past death's ground to new *Light* dear,
one in utter fear when the dark glass breaks—
The mirror to which you turn, by that you see—
So, to the Mount of our *cross-birth* Jesus came
to heal of the pitch poison hid in this world's mead—
Beyond fire's bane buds now flowering flame,
forked *lightning white*, our soul's bright tincture,
so fierce fire to *self*—Such the Son's *Love* tender—

THIS ROSE IS NOT A ROSE EXCEPT

This rose is not a rose except divine grace comes
amid such an imaginary *astral* bush of thorns—
Monstrous separator working in man's earthly mind
in false bestial will unable to find Thy will divine,
running and seeking again our first right native home—
Holy heavenly Hound of my ground's stirring grace
Come!
Again, the *Divine Ens* evanished in us awaken,
which loss left Man no more than a *Monster of Heaven*
leaving this whole visible world our enemy,
continually rent, scratched and torn with enmity—
Come restore—Breathe again into this hidden ground,
from above tender unto me my *God is Love* profound—
I, so blind to all Thy works, have no true understanding
to know myself and rest in Thee my only satisfaction—
So now from thy vast *Pacific Calm* breathe from above
of Thy mercy in awakened grace *swoosh down* like a dove—
Gentle Wind on-rest these waters whence all things are risen,
in Man God's *image* beget and speak flowing in thy *Chrism*—

AS I LAY UPON THE MOUNTAIN TOWARDS MIDNIGHT

As I lay upon the Mountain towards midnight,
so that all the trees fell upon me,
all the storms and winds beating with might,
Antichrist to devour me—O! His gaping maw
while searching for my native country to be free,
out of which this wearied soul had wandered long—
Hence my spirit from this thorny venture would flee,
ere to my ears came the Virgin Wisdom's song
to turn all these *mournings* dark into dawn—

I will *not* leave you in misery's plight,
but come to help you in the virgin's Son,
the most precious *Name Jesus* limned in your life's light—
For my Woman's Seed has the Serpent's head undone,
since budding forth out of Death's power, He won
in the promised sign's light, my Virgin's troth to you—
"I come to wed myself to you, that we may be *One*,
that God's *one androgynous Image* be renewed,
as Jesus' own inward Virgin Image knew."

MISERERE

When this wondrous knowledge arises, but nothing perfect,
know that my *Pearl*—Bright Lustre, I have laid aside
just as you, God's child of my Virgin's Wisdom, *He* hides
since worldly pleasures and Satan's assaults hourly beset—
You're cast into trial and vanity's mire, sin's debt
to sing *the Miserere*, and in humility reside
lest in your great *Joy your earthliness* my Beauty override,
imitating the Devil to your soul's eternal regret—
Once conqueror striking down the Evil One in the strife
take heed of fleshly pleasures, and in patience wrap yourself up—
Break the will and desire—bridle them as a horse untamed—
Then I will oft visit your fire with my *Love's Kiss of Life*,
for you are now a messenger of His Word incorrupt,
the Lord's instrument to resound his glorious refrain—

PURE UNDERSTANDING MOON

Thou pure and subtle understanding Moon
so darkened and clouded by reason of *drink*
while fullness of high feeding the body's buffoon,
so fake fasting's *silken robe* cast aside
at evenfall's brink,
that true as a toad out of honey poison sucks
like casting the evil ass up to the neck in mire
mute while your *Virgin* is lewdly lent out for hire,
your soul befouling itself as a swine swills muck—
But thou, *spirit of God's will,* e'er be in his Love—
Be growing forth out of stinging dung
as a fair flower—
Be sober—Give not *Brother Ass* bait he longs for,
but let it *fast oft* that your prayers be Dawn's
Winged dove—

BRIGHT LILY

Our brightness of Love so shut up in death,
corrupted, enkindled by the Devil cruel,
no longer with light in fire blessed
His forged tincture befouled our soul's best jewel,
for Adam's fair matrix of Venus was gone—
Our *mirror of Wisdom* a mere shade
in which Man's pure babe was to be born,
still God's dear image but some *doppler* made,
till the Champion strong in the combat came
surrounding Mary's spirit-soul with divinity,
putting taint, death and *Sheol* to shame—
His flesh and blood our Blessed Trinity,
this *Bright Lily* has again from death budded—
The whole Earth *now new* with his splendour flooded—

SIGNLESS

Upon waking up
the Soul found itself
fiery
circling round and round
the signless snowy woods
in great Distress
far from its nearby
Native Country—

KNOW THYSELF: *THE WILD HEIFERS*

The wonderful thing coming will begin *at midnight*
though many sleepers and drunkards will *not see it,*
yet the Sun will shine to the Children's delight—
Refulgent wisdom for the lovers of *Sophia*—
As his own heart and fabric God loves Man to surfeit,
like a Mother bearing a child out of her own substance
nourishes and leaves all her goods for it,
made in *his Image* and particular inheritance—
Without such considerations we live in blindness—

We run on as dumb beasts looking upon ourselves
and upon God's creation as *wild heifers* look
upon a new door made for their stalls, like rebels—
Ourselves against God—our will refusing to brook,
seeming strange, we start back refusing to budge a foot
and fall into this fearful darkness deep
because to know ourselves we will no effort put—
But there is none that can himself ignorance plead,
for *God's Will is written in our minds to heed*—

SAPPHIRE DAWN

Voice, once grey noise only— Sound's blaring son,
shrill heir to the *second fountain's* sharpness,
cold dark matter in the worm's gnawing brimstone,
fomenting in our five jabbing bitter senses,
till Christ's *Feuerblitz* to our hard essences came,
herald of the *fifth fountain's glance,*
this will's glad desire,
sounding *beauty of colours,* faith's sapphire dawn
Root sonata—
the Son's revolving angelic choir—
I was deaf— God's whispering lips I could not hear,
those three Splendours of his Voice
bruising the serpent's head,
his trumpet call opening the *Seventh Seal,* so dear,
till my Virgin Wisdom of wonders taught me to heed
faith's *sapphire,* hope's *gold,* love's snow *white*—
Mordecai's joys—
the *Ungrund's fifth fountain's* depth for the wise
to employ—

TENDER IT THE LOVE

Fair Rose, Virgin-Child in Paradise standing,
your fire-soul to its outward gross beast bound,
'neath the Cherub's fire-sword judgment turning—
So, tender it the love, your suppliant's sound
to forsake only the vain animal-man's ground,
laid up for it the labor of this weald—
This soul's true contrition's sorrowful bourn,
naught but naked-edged absolving sin till it's healed,
yet before you, *the Seed's Virgin-Child*, it yields—

This *Abscinder's* blade pierces your soul's heart,
abiding its entrance into sorrow for sins,
tossing vanity's weeds for the infant's shirt—
So, *Virgin-Bud* tender it the love, your next of kin
who bore you 'til the true Body's resurrection,
when grim death cuts off this bestial body—
thorny hedge and image of the serpent's *ens*—
Till then your soul stands 'neath Christ's Cross wholly
in sore straits of fiery continual cleansing—

White Rose, tender it the love in your soul's straits—
This orison raised for Noble Sophia's kiss—
In her beloved's trouble, the serpentine seed to abate,
her strength pure as refined gold to cherish
in the bitter struggle—this their marriage chalice,
taste of the sour wine, the soul's cross-birth

into sweet-light, the life of *His risen Presence*
'neath the Tree of Life, our new Heaven, new Earth,
and you in my arms, my *Pearl* of great worth—

A TERROR OF GREAT JOY

This is my flesh as bread to you I give
for the life of the world till the Last Day
when all which is eternal springs up again and lives
as your darkened mind's veil is broken and done away—
But for now my *Virgin Wisdom Body* turns to say:
Deliver me from the brimstone worm infecting my bridegroom,
and let me not be so *expired* as in some obscure tomb—

I am Thy ornament come for *You* to enjoy me—
Wherefore shall I stand with my bridegroom in the dark?
This harsh poisonous horror I long to flee,
for *divine Virtue* is my fair oriental *Pearl*—my mark,
my fountain of eternal bright light to impart—
But if he obscures my light, my garment defiles,
in my lost beauty, his worm will corrupt him and beguile,

so shall I lose my companion— my chosen bridegroom soul—
The holy *Seed of the Woman*, the Heart of God replies:
I break the *head of the Serpent*, the sour worm's control;
Dismayed at the meekness of my *Matrix*, it outward flies,
not changed, but a terror fleeing from great Joy descried—
Yet neither altering, not getting far from thence,
it raises aloft retaining its *galled* darkness,

terror making it a thin film from the *Fiat* harsh,
white lovely fire thrusting out that stern stifling death—

Gentle source of *Love* holding fast the Gall encircling the heart,
once wheeling anguish made into a veil by *the Flash*
separating pure and impure in this bold lightning breath,
as it drives the choking superfluity out,
and of its tough gluten makes an enclosure round about—

This night's cloak covering the *Love-Light* of the soul reborn
that may touch neither *Flash* nor *spirit*—this film, this gut
this turba banished forever from God's Kingdom—
It does not belong,
but as an outer dragon this black *ouroboros* thrust,
dissolving with death when our bestial body must,
even as this hard rocky earthly crust, the old creation,
outer darkness to *Christ in us*, our soul's incarnation—

MOST HOLY SWEET POWER

As the naked, blind, new-born kitten
mews for its mother—
Most Holy Sweet Power—
Highest simplest humility—
Relish of Love's goodness—
Sweet giving birth of
ecstatic delightful hearing—
Name Jesus—
Lovely Assurgency—
Holy Spirit springing into
One only Wisdom—
so our Soul cries out to Thee:
Purify my heart!

LYDIA'S SONG

That I might yearn for *You*, your flame wounded my heart—
I searched beyond all images, but *You* could not be found,
even out in the temples or public markets—
O teach me to understand my true longing's ground,
for my soul ever sought *You*, for this grace unbound,
to know and yield myself up to the *True One*,
by your *Inspoken Word* to be laid hold of and known

that I be opened to the fountain of this Love Divine,
the Sun of Life whence springs the heavenly water—
But the watchmen did not know my soul's love sublime—
As such a measure of grace to fulfill my hunger—
Then I was turned from where the watchmen wander
outside the city gate to the bank of the river,
and there heard your *Voice* in the words of a strange teacher

whose face as on a thorny bush seemed a rose so golden
in that burning bush which tongue sang of *God's Beloved*
with eyes so flashing that I could not look upon him—
There my spirit opened, and I found *You* whom my soul loves—
Stand still my heart as these waters spring from above,
your *Voice* penetrating deeper into this *ens*,
now the very hearer in me, this tinctured teaching—

Let me hold *You* near, my Lord, whose sweet name is *Jesus*—
Turning into this open door, I shall not let *You* go

until I bring *You* into my mother's house,
there to fill as a bower the abyss of my Soul,
the chamber of her who conceived me from Time Untold—
You, my soul's *Bridegroom* and I your *Bride*,
my eternities to your flowing majesty tied—

FIRE IN THE IRON

Essential flaming iron—
Bright fiery piece,
once so dark, hard and cold,
now so shining, so light giving—
See how permeated—so assumed!
Yet ceasing not *to be*,
but ever being iron—still free,
free, set in living flame consumed—
Bright flaming iron, yet ever the same,
Never hammered—Never shaped,
Never forged—Never quenched,
only receiving uncomprehending
this gently bellowing air,
the breathing heat—
Blazing radiance now replete
retaining only its propriety—
O Bright glance of *Majesty*!

Fire in the Iron—
Eternal flesh hidden
in the earthly Man—
Flesh Incomprehensible!
O thou bright *Crown* of *Pearl*,
brighter than the Sun
tincturing all *Natura*—
Word birthing a new Son

in the old man,
there is nothing like You,
Splendour penetrating my Soul,
so manifestly clear
yet so very secret,
though carried about in the breast,
scarcely rightly known, but dear—
Keep seeking and you shall find it—
Noble Precious Stone
in the fiery flaming heart set,
all joy therein to win
for the one to whom it itself unfolds
greater *Joy* than the world can apprehend—
No pen describing—
No tongue expressing—
None inquiring after
this trodden *Radiance*—
Yet only by the one who has it
is *It* ever known—
He seeks and all things finds
hidden in Heaven
hidden on Earth
this priceless *Rejected Stone*,
which all to powder grinds
and kindles *Light-Flaming*
Fire in the Iron—

ROCKING IN THE CRADLE

Our Mother cares for us
in whose bosom we live as children—
The garden of roses
our confidence and hope—
The precious herb our patience,
gloriously to be crowned,
Brighter than the Sun
fairer than the full Moon—
Yet far brighter and fairer
this *Pearl Tiara of Paradise*
set upon our soul—

We exhort you—
Enter into the bosom of *our Mother*—
Learn to see with your own eyes—
Suffer not the rocking in the cradle—
Desire not the eyes of others—
Strangers' eyes!
Rise up from the cradle—
Return to the *Mother*—
See our *Mother* and her children
and learn—
Speak from your own mouth—
no opinion from the mouth of another—
Sleep not!
Dream not the jugglers' dreams!

We lie supine in the cradle,
rocked asleep by dark hierarch hands,
seeing through alien eyes
the stars and their elements—
Our flattering caressing hypocrites
soothing with dissimulation,
hanging bells and baubles
babbling about our ears and cradles,
lulling asleep, fantasizing,
ever playing with dark baubles—
They the *By-Your-Leave Lords*
in this pilgrims' strange lodging—

O blind Reason!
Rise up from your rocking cradle—
Are you not our Mother's child, too,
an heir to the goods?
Child and true lord of the house
suffer not flattering servants
thus to use you—
defiling the *sacred silver temple*—

How good it is to see with your own eyes—
He, our *Morning Star*,
the Holy One who anoints us to know
daubs our eyes with his spittle
to apprehend the thing *As It Is*,
raising *Light of Red Dawn* in us,
seeing more than men as trees walking,
but transcending this shadow-life,

shining in the True Body—
So, triumph in our Spirit-Soul,
O thou Child of Eternity!

MOTHER OF PEARL

Anguish as a woman in travail, my soul,
aching for thy Light—breath of the Heart of God—
This fiery orb, so disquieted within, console
be like the Sun shining in the vast Deep
as the kindling of the quintessential stars,
birthed of the body of the abysm, my one seed,
out of the heart of darkness, *Light be*!
See this jarring first ground of twilight's longing,
prickle of *my will's desiring*, its attracting—

First sting, Love's unendurable first stirring—
Mother of my soul in the circle of the center
of such furious anguish— breaking whirling wheel
your light causes my *will's meekness* to long after *Light*,
but cannot reach it—cannot overcome—
So, come
Pillar of Lightning, terror to this harsh dark worm,
impregnate now with your twinkling flash,
your silent shriek and all cacophony soften,
all fierce pitch property vanquish

that my sunburst-struck mother be mild yielding-light
in the twinkling of an eye clear white,
trembling with great *Delight*, great desire—
Matrix of harshness from the flashing gleam
be essence of *no-thing*, eternity's attraction,

this fountain's soft and pleasant beams—
Nothing more full of refreshment, more fair,
gentle *watry* warmth, this End of Nature,
this perfection seeking nothing further—

PURE CHILD

Pure Child—
Eternal fire's extract
out of the sharp anguish,
from the worst
made best—
Lead our life—
Liberate from death—
Refine into
substance divine,
from the fire, Gold—
Remain unto
Nature's renovation
to the End
of this Time—

Pearl

MAGUS

Lord Christ, you came out of *Eternity into Time*—
I come back to you—Show me how to ascend—
Teach me to be thy *Magus,* I pray,
how to bring again into *Eternity Time's wonders,*
To change this dark night of faith's desire into Day,
this anguished source of death into life's luster—
Grant me thus the Samaritan's eyes and will
to know the Man to bear back to your Heavenly Inn,
restoring thy bright *Tincture* shut up in gloom
for the languishing, wounded, and half-dead to heal,
to dress and pour this soothing oil into all wounds—
Raise the dead, succor the sick, all diseases expel—
For thy honor, Lord, I openly set forth this *Pearl*—

PEARL

White my crystalline *Pearl* of the whole world,
oil sweeter than any honey can be—
What Lucifer and Adam off-hand hurled,
now from the crimson purple-red wrath set free—
Lover, if you knew what here lies hidden,
your only holy heavenly *tincture*,
how you would search to have, to hold unbidden
my cabinet'd treasures, Triumph's rapture—
Still from Paradise I bring you this garland,
I, *your Virgin* with tiara attired fair—
This in battle against the Devil and Death gotten—
But my *precious Pearl*, so sweet in the new birth,
how brave, how rare
white silvery-sound wherewith *I* crowned you,
I lay aside
till in our bower I am your Bride—

MARY

Mary! With all Eve's daughters earthly born—
Mary! Shut up maiden—our second Eve—
Just Adam's child of *the Covenant* shorn,
yet all Earth waits on your lips to believe—
Now this Earth appears bare, untouched as your womb—
No woman's *Seed* to bruise the Serpent's head,
no Virgin Bride to call our soul her groom—
Dare an angel's word move *mort* Heavenly Seed?
Yet Virgin Wisdom waits on your, "So be it,"
the *Word's Body* waiting in Everyman's vital Light
to sound once more our Father's chaste *Sophia*—
Name Jesus, our *Magnificat's* delight,
our soul swelling with your maternity,
our *spirit* streaming your virginity—

YOU BECAME MAN FOR MY SOUL'S LONGING

You became Man, my Lord, for my soul's longing,
to drink of your Spirit's water, life from above,
grace upon grace and gentleness now relishing,
springing from this fountain Wisdom, such cherished Love,
Heavenly flesh and blood, your own, my soul received,
your *Word* for my poor imprisoned spirit came
with your *Virgin* in pure essence conceived
in Blessed Mary, my own flesh and blood's frame—
Your blaze, my Lord, lights my soul's dark pyre
with *white clear light* of your *Love* burning—
this shared splendour's bright body of power
leaving your darling for *Paradise* yearning—
So be my Beloved, all my work, my life,
and I your nothingness, 'til I am your *Youth's wife*—

GOLDEN-SILVER CHILD

Pure Child, alphabet of nature's language,
eternal fire's extract of the sharp anguish,
from the worst made best—
Lead our life, liberate from death—
With your austere desire separate,
refine into substance divine,
remain unto nature's power, renovate
to the End of this Time—
Golden Child, desire of the Light,
Birth of highest degree tinctured bright,
turning round as this Earth
revolves, so this your eternal birth,
but now shut up is this your golden body
in the stony sable saturnine nature close,
black as a Raven in a dark cast
taking you into his earthly property,
upon you his *morning mantle* fastening,
upon your *Pearl* his covetous greed casting—
And though in his bowels he's no power o'er you,
no father to your essence of free desire,
your highest corporeity this fixed mortal incline,
where there is enclosing, yet no deathly transpire—
For when Death arises, you the Child are born anew
of the Heavenly essentiality Divine—
Child of liberty bruising the Serpent's head,
property of meekness, this first conception's stead,

out of *Goodness* and *humility*, sweet surrender
to *Luna*, body of the *Free Lubet's* desire,
gentle light's next of kin quintessential
birthed freely through death in the fire—
Become again the *Golden Child* out of tinctured *Silver*,
born in Man's true body of the *Crystal Temple*—

Luna then, arise from gold, transmute into whiteness
with your heavenly silvered-body arrayed
Cardinal virtues—three beauties of colours as *One*—
the Spirit's sapphire, Son's gold and Father's white as snow,
God's *Express Image* in Man of this Virgin Wisdom,
vailed in this life-time by the earthly Moon, though
in our bestial body's dark hardness hidden,
yet you are our true golden *God's Likeness*—

WE WERE ONCE MEN AND WOMEN

See Satan's *fell* fall like lightning from *Heaven*
to breech Adam—pure man, pure woman one,
to craven, to cut Man from his Maiden—
But to reverse death's sleep, God sent his Heart-Son—
He brought back to Man his chaste Virgin Wisdom,
circling our soul's ground with holy Love tender—
Our Father's fathomless Love-Body's kingdom
as we assume Christ's Virgin by surrender—
He our espoused, our Husband sworn,
We, Mary, in pure covenant begotten
from whom God and Man is cross-birth born,
her true body ne'er evanished nor forgotten,
timeless sign that we were once men and women,
thereafter love-bearing *chaste virgins to Heaven*—

EXCEPT FOR THE FAIR PARADISICAL ROSE GARDEN

I would not know saints who follow the Lamb,
Virgins reborn,
ashamed to bear on my pure body this naked
bestial form,
except for the fair *Paradisical Rose-Garden of Delight*
where man and woman are one body—like angels bright,
no longer abashed at this lonely ageing body to bear,
but ageless *man's fire* and *woman's light* to share,
not marrying, but bearing own love's androgenous fruit,
entering in to possess Paradise's eternal root—
Yet not only pure spirit, but with heavenly body shod,
full of chaste virginity, O *Sweet Image of God*!

THE SERAPHIC *KADOSH* OF WISDOM: *A FOOD TO THE DIVINE FIRE*

In the market places Wisdom raises her voice,
when the Spirit of God rises as a *Flame of Love*,
springing forth through your surrendering choice,
your soul's will-spirit descending from above
singing: "Glory to your name, Lord.
You are worthy, our God, to receive *virtue and power*,
honor, strength, wisdom and knowledge—Do as You will—
I can do nothing—I know nothing—I will go nowhere,
but only where you lead as your instrument, I dare.
Please do in and with me as You desire."

Now in the *tincture of meekness* throw your mind down,
expecting the Twenty-Four's casting their golden crowns
with angelic songs of praise and holy souls' "Selah!"
crying Hallelujah! Hallelujah! Hallelujah!
Light has dawned, so sing: "*Holy*! *Holy*! *Holy*!
is our God, Adonai Sabaoth!"
See this Spark of the Divine fall in complete abandon
into *Life's Center* kindling your soul's fire,
the light of divine power into flame there—
Now speak what the Holy Spirit whispers to you,
as you stand with this song—*Virgin Sophia's name*,
no more your own possession, but God's golden lyre—

MY BEING IS YOUR MOVING IN THE HEAVENS

My *Virgin Image*
break through
this half-slain essence
this shut up death—
Shiloh come
bring your *Chaste Sophia*—
Surround this Soul—
Quench all wrath
with your *Love-Light*—
Take me unto You
and lead me out,
then bring me in,
into these bright eternities—
You my fountain &
I, your sparkling Love drop—
My fullness this
my only being
your moving
in the *Heavens*—
You in me
and I in You—
One only desire
this blossoming
unfathomable *Body*—
This magical Marvel—

THE BODY BEAUTIFUL

Virgin Bride alone be our precious crown—
Clothe us with your ornaments and bright pearl,
all dangers for the Lily's sake to brave,
though a terrible tornado rage and imperil,
though Antichrist tear off the rags of the Woman
in our pain-bearing Eve's fleshly garment *bound*
to this earthly tabernacle till we send her to the grave—
Yet abide with us, *Virgin-Bride of our youth,*
betrothed, taken to each one of us as our very own—
Come be with your *bridegroom soul* at a time he desires,
as you wait upon all of Adam's homeless waifs
who have flung away, abandoned you like thieves in flight,
your *Virgin's tincture* now become earthly, almost dead,
waiting this whole time while Eve's flesh lives
in your stead—
Yet with yearning you call, admonish, seek to inspire
whether any receive you back into the new birth of faith,
women and men redeemed by birth-giving to *Christ,*
waiting with joy in your chaste *Body* till God
breaks this world—
Chaste *New Body* springing in our Lord's pure
Element's purl—

ADAM OF THE CRYSTAL SEA

You have taken my wearied soul upon your Cross
burning in this stuffed dark body of corruption's dress—
Yet for this breath ever of the eternal born,
a new heavenly body has been formed—
Sapphire-silver, out of the *pure matrix of the Earth*,
out of the Crystal Sea's substantial worth,
One blessed Element springing before the Father's throne,
your pure body prepared for me—flesh of the *Heart-Son* alone,
like Adam's first body—bright crystalline clear
has assumed into it my own soul so dear,
penetrating death—purchasing *it* out of death on the Cross
where You arise eternal restoring all things lost
where all things you saw and heard in me before
my own self willing, seeing, and hearing were adored—

I WAS EMBRACED WITH LOVE

I was *embraced with Love*
as his dearly beloved bride a bridegroom embraces,
like the Resurrection from the dead,
triumph in the spirit—no eye descries
no tongue expresses,
now gone way beyond that first perplexed
and exceeding trouble—
The deep melancholy
no Scripture could comfort or satisfy,
which my spirit elevated earnestly up into God
as with a great storm's onset and assault,
my whole heart, whole mind
wrapped up as in a mantle
wrestling with God's *Mercy*—his Love's sweet arrest,
not to give o'er until He *blessed*
with his Holy Spirit from above enlighten
virtue and power's reserve to test
all Hell's gates resolved to hazard even—
Then in the Light my spirit suddenly saw
in and by all creatures through all
beholding in this World's great Deep:
the Sun, the stars, the clouds, snow and rainfall,
considering the whole Creation replete,
finding in all things evil and good,
love and anger, in inanimate creatures: in wood
wind, stones, water, air—e'en earth's wide span,

all elements, so as in men and beasts,
why this little spark of light, Man, besides
should he be esteemed so in God's plan,
and that the wicked prospered
along with the virtuous and best—
Yet when in this affliction my spirit was lifted,
even in herbs and morn's dewy grass it knew
Who He is—how He is—and what His will,
my own *Will* suddenly set up until graced
to describe the *Being of God*—a mighty impulse grew
to write down this knowledge,
so with His Love embraced
so gifted—

ROSE GARDEN

I Thirst
with holy Love-thirst
tincturing in this heavenly blood
of my divine love
turning Adam back
in the *Deep-Sleep, redeeming*
your Virgin-like Image
from divided male and female
with this *Song* into
One
Masculine-Virgin
only in God's love
One
joyous glance only
into your loving *eyes*
sowing
our life-spirit *Seed*
of my fire
of your light
one tincture flowing
into the other—
Chaste Virgin
sweetness and wisdom
your fruit's delight
this Rose-Garden
this Something called Paradise

PEARL

your matrix of Venus
surrounding
my man-son's *limbus* of love
great joyous delectation
our conceiving
being pregnant with
another soul born
in God's Image
from our one-being
new-born from *One–*
It is finished
in the New Adam—

ONE LOVE'S MAJESTIC SHINING

It is the *End* of all creation,
so pour this water into fire's
essence of painful consuming,
this Love into wrath's
hidden hollowness called Hell:
My own self-comprehending—
My own painful devouring life—

For in Love
fire-terror's sudden shock
is our *In the Beginning*
of gentle, joyous Lightning's
brightness bearing
birth giving
crystalline water of fire and light
from the *Ungrund's* womb
one Love's majestic shining
Pearl of this whole new *Light-World*,
my Virgin Sophia—

STAR-DUST

Most holy sweet *Word of Power*,
pure soul from Mary's soul—
Open—Awaken with your knocking–
Call our hiding Lazarus
to arise, to come forth—
Voice of God from within,
this Nothing mortal
Nothing that beginneth
but the wonders only
sounding our one only *Oversoul*—
Its manifold tunes and voices
daily pouring out speech,
nightly revealing knowledge
heard throughout the Earth,
yet no speech, no words, no strain
our rational harmony before the Holy,
this substance *good*—substance *evil*
melodizing instrument of manifold frets,
this field of but One Life seething
holding *in common this*
spirit-dust of the stars and elements—
Silent-sea of voices proclaiming
our desires and wills multitudinous—
Yet, at the Last Day
You, my Lord, raise up
out of this One Body *of* Essences

our subtle bodies,
our many from this *One only*
sude in *Adam's numinous Soul,*
we, even as gods
living, moving, having our being;
Yet, all hearing one only *Voice*
of our *sweet first Mother's substance,*
this Nothing mortal
Nothing that beginneth
but the wonders only,
e'en the Son of Man's soul
walking in the cool of our evening
calling the souls *of All as one Soul*
to come forth—

DANCING WITH SOPHIA

O noble Lover, stand still
with your face turned towards *Me*;
Only *recall*, and give *Me* your rays of fire—
Don't withdraw, but with your thrust of faith
bring into *Me* your desire,
our joining hands in these rounds—
O *Infinite Vast Expanse*
bringing my rays of Wisdom, of Love,
my meekness into your fiery mind's essence,
these *great moments*—united with your forever—
And though we've never for an instant been apart,
but for this one thing and one thing only,
so in confidence again and again kiss *Me*
with the desire of your strength and power,
then shall I show you all my Beauty—
My liberation—all arising thoughts released:
You working your wonders in my Love,
shining brightness in your fiery life
of vivid wakefulness and emptiness this
our *one pure virgin thought* increased—

Invitation to the Dance:
It may be that your heart's desire, Dear Seeker,
hitch hiking through this World as in some Nevada Desert,
may wish to enter into our cherished inner choir,
through this door I've opened—this introduction,

standing still from your own self-thinking and willing,
your soul drawn in magically by God's *Love*
into that out of which the world was made,
you, too, joining hands and *Dancing with Sophia*—

STAND STILL WITH YOUR FACE TOWARDS ME

Stand still
instrument sweet
noble Soul
turn your face
Look at Me—
Don't fall asleep! But
bring your desire,
enkindle Me
O rays of fire!
And take Me,
Begetress sublime
with my meek beams
harmony divine,
my *Love* consummate
with your fiery mind—
How well I am
joined with you,
O my bridegroom—
Stand still
and kiss Me again,
desire's bestowal
of your strength
in *Love's* abandon,
your Power—
Then magically in
our birth-giving

you I'll show
all *My Beauty*—

137

THE TIME OF THE LILY

My bridegroom, at a time before you call me to you,
I sometimes visit when you desire my play,
if your fleshly senses and thoughts do not hinder,
then your *dark night* shines as brightly as the Day,
as I would fain return again, my place not eschew—
But your Virgin will not be bound to an earthly center,
for to *my lover* only I appear in *high triumph*
diving into the tincture of the blood of your heart,
that your body, mind, and senses so highly tremble
as if you were in *The Paradise* to play its will's part—
And though I with you may *not* stay continuously,
for not in earthly vessels dwells my high birth,
I always carefully anticipate and call you first,
which you may only understand in my *fragrant Lily*—

RIDING IN THE CHARIOT OF THE BRIDE

Heaven's silent healing herb of the sacred hour—
God's blessed love in the light thoroughly shine,
be our precious refreshment from Christ's own flower,
herb hardly found upon Earth by men's incline,
only on the forbidden Tree's poison dining
in the fierce wrath of our eternal nature—
But come *Everyman* to the Mercy of God's designing,
forsaking all of the foreign outward creature
for your soul's gentle Bride, Christ's eternal nurture
ere the Creation when it was purely a seed—

Come if only for *that moment* where no creature dwells—
Come hither and find your *Creator-Word* and feed—
Eat of that humanity which all sickness quells—
Ineffable words of meek pure love, *God's Spell*—
There your soul receives the Holy Spirit's entrance
in your spirit's standing still from all self-will
to dine on the *Heart-Son's* flesh, his puissance,
your drink—joining hands in *Sophia's dance*—

The sweet *Word of Power* said to Lazarus, "Come forth!"
The dead must arise, awaken with his knocking—
Hearing God's Voice within be your *Last Day's* comfort,
his tinctured sound blessing your mind from all self-thinking—
Then of this intimate and indigenous working,
this embrace in the *cross-birth* of your will-spirit's center,

hear my child in your sweet surrender, the Lord's speaking
in eternity as your *golden likeness* enters
into the blessed Bride's body of Christ's splendour—

Inwards herein be so refreshed, so released,
and plunge your mind into that where no creature is,
pressing forth with its yielding will in the midst,
presently to be clothed upon with supreme *Bliss*—
tasting in yourself the *Inspoken Ungrund* of Jesus,
the joys thereof no tongue's words can supply—
In this Virgin's beams know your *spirit's tinctured abyss*—
No such splendour can the mind conceive as the soul rides
ascending and descending in the *Chariot of the Bride*—

INTIMATE AND INDIGENOUS

I propose as an intimate and indigenous work
this practice of pure faith to turn mountains upside-down,
this healing herb rarely to be found upon the Earth—
For in feasting on just the forbidden Tree men abound,
not true surrender in the Father's tender bosom—
But your spirit-soul riding in the Chariot of the Bride
masters all in the will of the Holy Spirit's motion
as there your own will's *inward man's* transmutation hides,
there is nothing can be named that it cannot subdue
introduced into the outward man this inward cure—
Jesus Christ's *power* to God's holy children imbued,
being the thorough-shining Love of God in Light pure—

THAT BY WHICH GOD SAW AND HEARD IN YOU

Into Heaven's *great moments of silence* throw yourself,
where no creature dwells even for a moment—boldly
stand still from thinking and willing of *Self*
and you will hear the words of God unspeakable, holy
before nature was, you are as God, quiet and convinced,
hearing and seeing with that by which God in you, saw and heard
even before your own seeing and willing commenced,
now stopping the influx of *cold dark matter's* force to disturb
that binds you and keeps you in your own self-made fierce prison—
Thus, submitting your mind to the *cross-birth*—your soul bow-down
and go out thence to that supra-sensual horizon,
the renewed nature of your right eternal ground—

THE FELLOWSHIP OF HIS SWEET INTERCEDING

By a quiet introversion and secret communion,
for even a few moments your own will breaking
in the great Love of God your spirit and mind's submersion,
the most holy sweet power of the *Name Jesus breathing*,
wrap your soul in the *Pearl's* joyful recollection—
Descending and ascending in Christ's white bridal garment,
finding here all things and assumed in One Glory,
recalling your will-spirit's anointed enlightenment
into the abyssal Mercy *of* God beyond all fear
into the sufferings of our Lord Christ and *remember*
the fellowship of his sweet interceding—how endeared
to see and hear the *Father's Love*—unspeakable Splendour—

THE THOUSANDTH

The tincture is master, while your soul gives the thrust
in this remembrance of the Lord Christ's choosing you,
thus shall your countenance shine again as pure water must—
Cleansed, you shall then hear God's *Voice* with purity imbued,
drawing tincture's rays from inward to the outward man:
Raise the dead, heal the sick, and all diseases expel—
Naturally, only God's Spirit rules over the *turbic* band,
so, as his humble child under this *cross-birth* stand still,
overpower death—working your wonders in Christ's love dear—
For in this eternity's practice there no death stands,
bridling the Devil who rules in its fierce fear—
This *Love's* discipline—stronger than all things, Commands—

MAGIA

Magic my mother
leading *Light-of-Life*
be mine own
striving in the will-spirit
towards the Heart of God,
tincturing this water-gently
entering into meekness-softly
into our *Ternary's desire*, e'en
Majesty's flame making flesh divine—
Yet—
Desiring of all beings,
Nothing but one will,
be my fire also—
Desire me burning in
your eternal magical fire
a very yearning fire
a perpetually finding fire
something into *no thing*
no thing
but
all *essences* ours
in *Virgin Wisdom's* looking-glass
hungering for the *Heart-Son*
desire's austerity
purging this floor,
finding my ending,

only leaving
these ashes of dying—

IRIDIUM: *THE MAGICAL BEGETTING*

We should have given birth
to a Virgin-Image,
to our joyous conception
with my *soul's* fiery eye
resolved, beholding
your *spirit's* gentleness and love,
its looking back into—laying hold of
the *love of life* in mine—
But I could not,
only turn away from
your *New World* waiting
in the light of your eyes cradling
our Christ-Child, Jesse's Root
swaddled in our virgins' vast chorale
singing the *Lamb's Song*—
But *our morning's womb*
I shut up in Death—
turning this fiery yearning away
from you, O *Bride of my Youth*,
from our *magical begetting*,
toward the animal frolicking phantasy
bestial in two fleshly bodies,
three-time divorcing you, *divided*,
till *He* who flourishes like the Juniper
this human half-slain essence
invited in

Bringing back with Him
your Virgin Chastity's warm *Iridium*
surrounding my fiery soul
allaying the wrath left in this void,
apprehending my Man's tincture
once more
with your gentle meekness
His glance of Love—

THE CRYSTALLINE SILVER TEMPLE

O Man! Find this pearl and look Moses in the face,
for no flesh as we now bear can live in God's Heaven—
Thus, our heavenly flesh before the Fall's disgrace
took its food from the seed of the Spirits *Seven*,
and from a nobler ground took Earth's essential leaven,
an extracted mass out of the sacred *Salniter*—
For when *Nature's* vast body was kindled by Satan,
then God's Heart molded a mass for Man's outer figure
ere the corrupted *Salniter* was pressed together—

Today because of its hard fierceness called Earth,
this limbic mass, till *Day Six*, stood in the dark deep Vast,
when God's *Heart-Son* breathed the *Light of Life* in birth
into the innermost or *third birth* in the Mass,
where the Seven Fountain Spirits' seed gave birth at last,
thus, Man became a living spirit-soul eternal—
So, think not that before his *Fall* Man had members crass
to propagate with, but paradisical,
nor entails or stink as Man's bodily externals—

But *Man* was created immortal like the angels—
Born out of the *Limbus*, he was pure—God's very pearl,
holy extract at the Fall of the host of devils,
an angelic host again to give to this World—
Know that God made him not of the Earth's lumpy burl,
but created his true body a quintessential mass

out of the stars as their elements unfurled—
Yet this *tincture* was of the *holy matrix* amassed,
as the Moon's property shines with a heavenly cast—

Behold! Man's true outward body is in like manner
kin to our inward body's habitation and mansion
before the Fall—a *watery-crystalline silver splendour*,
fluent seed from the *pure portion* of Earth's partition
in the Judgment to be cut *from* the Earth's condition
in the curse—from corruption and vanity,
to see the pure element's *Spiritual Man* within,
one of two streaming nuclei in Adam's *fixity*—
Behold! Our *Love-essence's* elemental body,

this *outward Heaven*, once God's *silver temple pure*,
fire and light in beauty's colours if not tarnished now,
these two mutually espoused to each other secure
formed as *One Soul-Body*—most holy tincture endowed
divine fire and light in great Joy's tender abound—
The inward as its sensation loved the outward,
ardor's tenderness for one another to redound—
The outward as its greatest sweetness loved the inward,
both essences ardent for each other without words.

joyous silvery pearl and most beloved spouse only.
yet they were not two bodies, but only one pleasance,
a two-fold marrow, one inner and most holy,
the other from the watery crystalline essence
espoused and betrothed to each other ever precious
as the beauty of colours through and round both begirt
inward and outward stirring up heavenly Venus,

both seeds of man and woman joined in great joyous mirth,
the Son and Virgin's *express Image, our* magical birth—

BELOVED COMPANION

My Lord and living *Word*,
where You are there am I,
your Virgin-Wisdom, your *Love*
ever *being* in me,
here in your *eternal Pearl*,
not one *of us* without the other,
else behold eternity divided—

My *Beloved Word*,
when you entered Mary's matrix,
the *Fiat* in her flesh and blood
opening her eyes to behold
my wonders, your own *expression*,
all her essences, her faculties longing
ever cried out for the *Living God*—

My *Champion Leader*,
you attracted her flesh
into my Virgin *Eterne*,
your true Soul of Christ
coming forth out of her maiden's
now pregnant yearning—
The perished soul of Adam
shut up in the death of the holy *Ens*,
now in her body
set once more our Heavenly humanity,

our *blessed among women* conceiving
You in me in our Father's *Virgin Mind*—

Behold! God *is* become Man,
and I, human substance
with your human soul,
your very divine *Image of God in me*,
and You in me, Man's *Beloved Companion*
in Man's living vital light—

The Father's *Heart-Son* in the cross-birth
is come into an earthly Mary,
and I in her,
Love's *Wisdom holy* in the Trinity of God—
For You, my Lord, have ever been in me,
your Virgin *in Ternario Sancto*,
myself your body,
your own Heavenly Body
flowing from your bloodied crown of Majesty,
from your wounded limbs and side,
piercing Mary's heart, saying,
This is your Mother—

You, my Lord, in the living center of the Tree
in the *Holy Ternary*
for all those who receive You,
who believe in *our Yeshua*,
to be mine own companion, and even
be Mary in the Covenant of Grace
bearing my *Beloved Word* become flesh—

THE YIELD-LIGHT CONSTANT

When I see an herb standing
in the Beginning
1 *only* fragrant fashioning
blooming in its essential-oil spirit
tincturing root of Nature's Joy—
Number 3
in Ternarius Sanctus
lovely blossoming bouquet
signaturing—O beauteous colours!
Thou forming shaping beholding
of 7 forms' dimensionless egress
through all that's coagulated & coarse—
O Earth, Earth, Earth!
United with the *Unity*
See
One with all things,
Comprehend by grace,
O take your delight, your longing in
all things coming into being
in high holy principle pressing forth,
proportional harmony's
innate and instant generating
penetrating & rising
this *angeli mundi*
overcoming love-wrestling
whence paradisical powers rejoice

standing in this *7th Birth*
hearing the Word of the Lord,
in sacra lingua naturae
of taming gentleness
passing through and out purely
the fierceness of vanity's death—
Merely this *Yield-Light*
imprinting with your primal efflux,
with your tone articulating
fragrance, form and color forth-coming,
naming all things,
but not in the Latin tongue,
just naming your children—

THE DOE

The doe rested the night
'neath Fall's willowed bower,
on its leaves and flowers fed—
Gracious Lord, your call
like gentle rain comes slow,
subdues our will, our might
in *Man* and in creatures all—
She lay there *still*—the grassy bed,
while chewing the cud,
taking her rest,
a wary watch changed to loveliness—
For all things gladly give their will,
to the *Light of Life's* power yield—

THE ENCHANTED BUMBLE BEE

As still as the enchanted Bumble Bee lounging on its lavender sweet,
so in thy Death, O Christ my Lord, my quieted spirit rests,
when my keepsakes six groan—passing into their last gasping cry
Crescendo the Wrath in my rotting flesh—pieces to putrefy—
Death throes in life's last sonic boom—now the inner ear's mere beep—
Woman, this is thy Son—*John, care for thy Mother—Do not weep!*
I am the Deathless—
Calling the high angelic role—called up out of humanity's flesh,
choosing the *Golden Silver* children of the *limus terrae*
to dance upon the Earth's May of Man transfigured into Heaven,
the mirror of Majesty's wonders appearing therein—

UPPER CROSS

How fair and surpassingly excellent is thy splendour
conceiving white crystalline water of *Heaven's firmament*,
flaming *love-body* of Venus' own fine lineaments,
praise unto thy great meekness and sweetness we surrender
to heavenly fire's *breathed on oleus* flow so tender,
thou sweet spiritual essence in the new birth's sacrament,
poured out power of our *Samuel's Hand* upon the penitent,
the soul's new white-water body, a mansion rendered
of great sovereign power, the Son's Gethsemane press,
Love-Desire's brimstone oil of his heavenly blood,
whence from our bad thorny bush fair rose-buds bloom from
darkness,
this noble image, shut up in death, redeemed 'neath God's tender
flood,
and Man, once fair blossom and fruit of Paradise, redressed
dear *fifth form's Pearl*, where long only a bestial, dead image stood—

YOU HAVE CLOTHED THE NAKED

You have clothed the Naked,
Supra-imaginal Lord,
Sovereign substantiality—
Behold this investiture Supreme!
I was already resting in my bed,
early listening to the murmuring *Neisse,*
yet You put your *Hand* through *an empty door,*
calling to my desire, to press after—
But why should I be roused and rise up,
just walk out to leave my imaginary dream-life?
O! To be quitted of such a low condition,
put above images, figures, and shadows,
o'er all creatures great and small rule,
reigning in the very ground of that reunion,
receiving *no Thing* into this will's desire,
nothing on Earth to harm my being
a simple Child purely petting
all things red in tooth and claw,
your power and wisdom threefold glittering,
Seraphic fervor rousing them to meekness,
my being now like them all,
and nothing unlike me,
as a Child-regent, Prince of God,
vested with that *pure and naked knowledge*
Supra-imaginal—

JUPITER SPARKLING SPRINGING UP

Gentle *Lightning Flash* into your wheeling carousel
springing up of life, so soft and clearly shining
sweet *dry-water* as I walk out this empty door of
my doomed house of *Red Dawn arising in the East,*
where I shall *spring up* in this morning's Paradise
as *You* bear and rejoice in all things with your sparkling
infinitely wafting colours—absolving arts,
powers and virtues of eternal awe-filled wonders
love-wrestling—showing themselves endlessly
pageanting more and more, wonderful and marvelous
merrily as you go round moving, carrying
your little laughing lovely children—wide-eyed
angels of this garden of delight and pleasure
as they play with the erstwhile wild animals
gleefully riding on the friendly leaping lions—
Others petting the meek *marmots* whose shadows alone
are feral, biting, but now subdued, submerged
walming 'neath your caressing turning about
whispering— Rest my little *kinder* and creatures,
for it's the *Seventh Body,* the Holy Sabbath—
See our mother aerial-watry *Light-World*
softly flowing kindly over the *Neisse,*
over and round your evanescent country cousin
as it gurgles past this scorning Goerlitz,
gilded and blind fleeting thorn in my flesh—

But you are my One only essential soothing psalm,
balm and flowing fountain issuing from God's Main,
the dear *Heart-Son's* will of our tender Father,
Lord Christ, your Spirit, the crystalline choreographer
for these maying slow-motion rounds
pollen-laden among the Linden *tilias*—
For you are the separator pure, the dying
to our cold dark hard Western *sude*
rudely hidden 'neath those capricious countenances,
those boiling, seething powers of Nature's elements
oft hurrying noisily past our house where
I've recently had the smashed windows replaced—

But you just saunter by whistling a tincturing tune
as you have not a worry in this whole World,
valiant *Eternity* scintillating through voracious *Time*
with heavenly hands in the gates of your deep pockets
the Eternal Spirit's signature in your *walming*
vast virginal *Body* of the *One pure Element*
opening out with magic fingers welling,
brandishing *Jupiter's* lavish water-color brush
tincturing the liquid-air with unfolding strokes of Beauty—
This *One* essential Kingdom of goodness and splendour,
springing forth dancing *New Salnitral Earth*,
waylaying the darkness of this worldly *astrum*,
sacra lingua budding and blossoming of all things,
glowing seeds now growing limned of fiery light,
our Father's *Virgin Wisdom* and *Love's Delight*—

And as I pause at mid-bridge for a moment,
musing prior to passing to the other side,

I know that Katherine will be patiently watching
bravely abiding, awaiting my return home
from this another summons to the Town Council
to gainsay the *Primarius's* charges—

THE CHAMBERED NAUTILUS: *COMING TO THE LIMIT*

Desire, will-spirit's hunger for the Heart of God,
behold *Him*, and in death do not die—
Pass through death's fierceness with splendour shod,
through the glass darkly into Love's fire hie!
Divine *Magia*, mother of eternity's supply,
directrix of wonders in the *Great Mystery*,
this seething maelstrom she guides you by
to enter into her mirrored facsimile,
pure antidote to death here your *first face* see,

your true *tincture*, nacred pestilence to Hell,
holding it captive, dire *sude's* surcease—
Only then to surely taste, to fully feel
all prurience shed once you're past death's embrace,
to behold your three magical mirrored face
viewing in the glass each other's founts
cascading opening this wondrous *glance of faith*,
one joy clasping another joy to surmount
wordlessly whispering great *Love-Ens* redoubt

washing o'er *turba's* tintinnabulating knell—
Delve deeper in beholding *hope's joyous glance*,
letting all other go, now lift back one more veil,
this gently winding *nautilus* limns your advance
to find the beginning and the end, your true manse,

all seeking and pain's source now cast away—
Yet with boiling *sude's* poison, still perchance
each precious puissance fair stands to captivate
till you unfold *Third Heaven's* tongueless articulate,

facing God's pure *Love*, your spirit's last turning round,
no destroyer dare near this greatest bliss of all—
White as snow, standing dauntless *Death be not Proud*
when no more pain abides in this abyssal
Pearl, where your will rests in itself withal
in nothing else, but its own native mind,
continuing deeper in, comprehending all
in this *Beatrice*, conducting spirit sublime
further into *the Limit* to finally find

in your bestial body's fall no lamenting,
your soul no longer feeling its baleful burden,
but only for the lovely burning now longing,
wishing for the wonders of that which it has been—
So, bereave not this animal body of sin,
for the fabric of your soul's fiery orb—
That beginning glowing faculty does not dim,
but if *fell*, passes into dark shade, is absorbed,
except your graced spirit be with God's splendour robed

with Christ's Body, *Chaste Sophia's* pearl wedding gown—
Then your *lily-twig* now blossoms true
by its meek heavenly body pure *Love Ens* crowned
with the Holy Spirit's *living flame* imbued,
you've no memory of the former life to rue,
no burning in mental anguish or great horror,

only *born from above*, blessed with flesh divine's purlieu,
swallowed in eternity's *magia*, *Majesty's* desire,
your soul burning ardently in God's Love-fire—

165

THE PEARL IS IN THE JEWEL

Keep seeking if you do not understand this writing—
Don't as in Lucifer's pride, fall mocking and deriding,
but for the humble lowly *Heart-Son* of God seek—
That will bring a small grain of mustard seed,
then fruit from the *Tree of Paradise* into your soul,
and if you in patience abide, a great tree there will grow—
Father, it pleases thee to hide these things from the wise,
for thy babes and sucklings on *Virgin Wisdom's* breast rely—
Therefore, seek in the *Jewel* for the *Noble Pearl*—
It is much more precious than this whole world,
and it will never ever from you depart,
for where the *Pearl* is, there also will be your heart—

You needn't hunt any further seek but the noble *Pearl*—
Then when you find that, *Paradise* you at once retrieve,
and so are taught, for without it you cannot believe—
You may labor in art and science for *Wisdom* fair,
for her depth and height, yet she hides not there—
The doctorate without this *Door* knows her beauty not,
for in the way of gentle meekness is her mead got—
What is lacking here that you long after? Seek further—
Find in your ground's yearning the *Pearl of the whole world*—

NOBLE BURNING WHITE

Noble burning White
blossom of Love's desire,
out of fierce Death
in this soul's dark fire,
as a flower
out of Earth's bosom
as the apple receives
the virtue of the tree
though *quite another thing,*
another will conceive,
rekindle the *holy*
light flaming fire—
Image beyond Nature,
yet ever still there
standing in
your abyssal root,
even as Majesty's Sun
also giveth *virtue* unto you,
noble burning
White Clear Light—

THESE GREAT MOMENTS: *ON THE REBIRTHING OF THE HUMAN SPIRIT*

Adam's timeless piece
clockwork *Virgin* figure
set by the *Finger of God*
in the Deep Center—
Matrix of innumerable wonders,
her three moments always striking,
one magically begetting another,
Incremental dark nights between
each light-flaming divine essence,
this spirit-soul's wheeling constellation,
non-being of all beings,
your own possibilities—
One *Mercy* measuring out another,
conceiving from the Father's
love-desiring all souls
in your masculine-Virgin
out of your luminous likeness,
this endless knowing,
this token of arising victory,
each *mysterium-mirror*
modelling the other,
bringing forth its *first-born*
each new *Image of Man*
for our Joy and Delight
this vast human host divine—

FIRE OF GOD'S LOVE DRAW ME

Fire of God's love draw me into your Last Judgment Day,
fiery attraction into your substance alone dear,
this Body Divine through anger through Death convey—
Christ, my Shephard, in your crystalline flesh and blood clear
teach me to yield after love's manner, teach me to burn,
in this gross body, hid *power and virtue* cherished
with no limit nor end, for your abyssal world's return,
Paradise springing, blossoming with all hardness perished—
But fire's torment—what I wrought in dark anger,
the soul penetrated as a burning hot iron possessed,
immediate judgment at this dead body's departure,
for in such my soul cannot come to your *Sabbath Rest*,
except in Thee, who stands and delivers me from mine own *Hell*,
myself now Heaven in your *Love's flaming fire*, God's *Will*—

HOW FAIR NOW THE PINE TREES OF LEBANON

How fair now the pines of Lebanon,
whispering softly to me of our old *Mother*,
of our native country—
So, let us speak of great wonders,
how all things are going with you,
that I may set it down for the *Lily-Rose's* sake—
Then together we may comfort ourselves,
for we are *strangers in this strange land*
Let us persuade one another and agree
to go home to our country, our *Mother*—
O how she will rejoice
when she sees her children
hurrying home to her
passing through the ancient gate,
coming to her into Eternity—
We will tell her our stories
of our awful afflictions
which we suffered in Jericho—
We will speak of the great danger we were in
among the many evil beasts—
We will sing a song of the dread Driver,
and how he is now *captivated*
after holding us so long hostage,
who plagued us day and night—
And we'll rejoice to relate

how we were set free from him
by paying *faith's royal earnest penny*,
our open gate into the *Garden of Roses*
with lilies and flowers enough
to weave our *Virgin Sister* a garland,
regaling in Noble Sophia's rounds
joyfully holding hands
with no more might to harm us,
our *Mother* feeding us 'neath the Fig Tree,
our hearts holding no more contradictions
o'er-flowing with Wisdom's fruit—
How fair now the pines of Lebanon,
whispering sweetly to me
'til we all meet together in Zion
rejoicing in eternity's rhythm
flowing through the *Last Day*—

SET THIS HEART ON FIRE

Blood of love's desire
set this heart on fire—
Inspeaking flood welling
from your wounded side
Breath of grace divine
wash away this hardened willing—
This self-willed serpent's poison
desiring into animal vanity
of my own rights mattering
harboured here—

Blood springing up from
the holy *Ens* of love
set this heart on fire
with your *Inspeaking* grace,
your *Voice* in motion remain
until this world expires—
leaving merely this Fountain of Life,
holy tincturing of the Pain
changing it into *Joy*—

PRAY NAKED

Come down here, lowly in this *dust*—
Sit with me
lest your own understanding exalt you to *Hell*,
for I lie down in the Courts of my God
at His feet—
Come down here, *to sleep to your self*
'til His Spirit wake you,
and if He will not
only look up to Him in *solitude*
into your soul's wrestling
'til the *dark night's center* break,
'til a noble *Lily-Branch* sprouts
void of understanding
humbled *fool* to all reason
wrestling like Jacob
'til the breaking *Red Dawn* mounts
in the East when your *son* is born,
Herod standing ready with his sword
with outward persecutions
in inward temptations
to try whether the strength
of this your *Lily-Branch*
be stalwart enough to destroy Satan's domain—
O *Serpent Destroyer*
brought into this *still* wilderness
after your Baptism with the Holy Love-Spirit,

tempted, tried in surrender's fire to God's will—
O Soul, stand still to all earthly things,
your spirit's eye shut to alluring *cold dark matter–*
Come down here—
Sink into nothing
Attract nothing
Imagine nothing
and sit with me, God's Fool
praying naked in the dust
in the Courts of my God
at His feet—

HIGH LIFE: *THE NIGHT WATCH*

High *Life*
irradiating *Wave*
Initiate—
Dispose this mind to receive
Nothing and All Things—
Cast *Me* overboard
into your swelling *Deep*
down unto this wee hours' *abyss*
this little space of *Silence*,
deeper still to conceive
where no creature dwell
to recollect this *spirit's* will,
the earnest of my *vows* to keep
in the *bowels* of Thy *Presence*
only to remember *Thee*, my Lord,
just to hear *Thy Voice*—

Jewel

LOVE YOU TAKE ALL: *TO THE NOBLE VIRGIN*

Love, You take all,
all of this poor soul taken possession,
being in trouble—being in pain—
For if in trouble you dwell not
you'd have nothing to love
with your *Love's living flame,*
surcease of this *self's* sorry lot,
Burning now her own will yielding
till she yearns to herself to die
to expire,
to be *Nothing* rendered—
For where *Nothing* dwell,
there you, my Lord of Love, reign
never to leave, nor forsake or distain,
but to go with me in your ransoming fire
destroying Death's proud ground—
For even if my soul into darkness sank down,
you'd for your Darling's sake harrow Hell—

Love, You take all,
that this soul's Beloved alone
again you might be—
For what you are could never be known
without *Something* for you to love—
Your *virtue* alone that no-thing
whence all things arise—

Your *power* all things enthrall—
Your height as high as God—
Greatness even greater–
For whosoever finds *Love*
finds nothing
finds *All*—

OUT FROM THE VERY HEART: *A MANDALA SHIELD*

Out from the *Very Heart*
in the twinkling of an eye
in a moment
kindled in the midst
out from *The Deep* of the body
rising out and up aloft
out of the *heat* of your heart
the *right spirit* speaking
the Word of Light
when you proclaim it,
going forth flowing
going forth suddenly
like a flash of lightning
as the spirit's heated kernel
kindles in the sweet quality
in the midst of the *Son of God's* birth—
Hertz!
Most Holy Sweet Power, Name Jesus
Joyful flash of the Lightning of Life
shine in the terror of darkness—
Release my spirit, soul, and body
from the Evil One
who rules in the corruption of matter—
Shine into all the powers
out of darkness and death's shadow

breaking apart the bonds that hold,
even as the Sun does in the whole world—
Go forth from the fierce bright-burning
Clarity,
Thou Holy Love-Spirit
Go forth, O *Brightness of the Son of Man,*
out from the Very Heart—

SOUL FOOD

As the little dog waits under the table for the scraps to drop—
As the cat, fearing the heat, circles the pot of hot broth,
so does *Man* enjoy the paradisiac fruit,
and Christ's *new birth* enter, unless he leave Adam's skin,
cast off reason's flesh, and into rebirth's circle enter in—
For all the *flora* that humans now eat poison the body,
all being descendants of the *Knowing Astral Tree*—
But our soul comes from the eternal magical fire,
its globe-like blaze feeding on *God's Love*,
gentleness and essence,
reborn imaginating into *Love*, its waxing crescence—
As the flame's desire searches for the heart-wood,
my soul longs for the true Manna, the Heart, *the Living Word*,
dining on the same food as is the holy angel's fare,
just as our Father his *Heart-Son's children* ever desires
from *eterne to eterne* with tender loving fire—

OUTSPOKEN

Out of the *Heart of God* going forth endlessly
open wide the *Gates of the Deep* in this mind—
Forming and framing all, love-wrestling wheel sublime,
not when and how I will, but by your *Crown of Majesty*
you open wide or shut, no one denying your decree,
with your seven spokes radiating eternity's time,
else not our least sparkle up to the fellied Godhead climb
where the desirous kindled Spirit is that Crystal Sea—
Then what makes us so zealous-burning like a fire
as these four wheels gently gyre without ever turning,
except the precious *Virgin Wisdom* meeting us to inspire,
saying:
I am thy Bride in the Light my attracting your yearning,
my Gate of Knowledge and glory your illuminate quire,
with this form espousing myself to you, my Pearl adorning—

THE TEACHER

Arise—
Take wing
thou understanding spirit,
O Sun of splendour's
Glance—like lightening
Speak wonders—
Un-divide—
Our *Body* make whole—
Enkindle—
Into *Mercy* press—
The Wild Vine
trim and dress—
Enlighten—
Plant into the Divine—

COME FORTH GENTLY

Come forth gently
O Seven fountain Spirits,
well up into this tongue,
as sweet-sounding water captivate—
Shine, *O Birth of the Light*
with your *flash* of soft ringing,
let this speech articulate clearly
what from this world's beginning
is not revealed to any man's sight—
But if in this corrupted flesh,
temperate tempest that you are,
this lightning thought pure
from the band of nature be set free,
then this *spirit-body* could see and know
shining in splendour—*Light of Majesty*,
then this bestial form
it would resemble no more,
but to the angels of God be conformed—

IF ONLY MY SPIRIT DID SIT IN YOUR HEART

Lead, my Lord, all the vanquished foes in triumph
as this *fifth fountain's flower* from our earthly sheath springs up
out of God's vast Pacific calm as sweet as cream
midst *cold dark matter* and bitter driving forms now beteem,
out of the very heart of darkness and death
behold *Thy Love—Thy Joy*,

not like a man who rubs rock and wood—with heat his prime employ,
like Lucifer's legions elevated and so hard compressed,
that hellish fire of God's wrath framed his only reward,
whence the sweet fountain of water in them dried up,
where once the light kindled, wherein love erst rose up
twixt *compressor and dark energy* came the sour rank heat,
pride's deceit and fierce grasping greed
fouling the flowing water sweet—

But when *Life's Light* came—my Lord's bright azure *Faith* from Heaven,
dissolving bitter hardness, *Meekness* brighter than the Sun,
once dark ground, now arisen dear *Clear Light* gifts to Man,
so pleasant a life, this wellspring of Love's vast span—
Lily-Child, if only my spirit did sit in your heart
and sudden spring up, then your body would leap as with a start,
else you cannot apprehend, nor I bring it to your sense
unless God's Spirit spark your smoldering soul's reticence,
then in your *free will* shall this lovely *Light* be born—
Rise up in bitter cold, *Sweet Triumph*, this spirit-soul adorn!

THE SCENT OF WILD ROSES: *REPLY TO ARNOLD'S DOVER BEACH*

Love, come to the Virgin's mirror—Come see dawn's rising for us—
Behold! This *never gone gleam* shining forth from the Hidden One,
Root of our five senses, eternal life's victory won,
God's *Word of Power Scientia vincere tenebras*—
Listen! Hear the Ocean's breathing forth our desire's *faith*,
the Holy Love-Spirit's joyfulness—this high revelation
calling Man's twisting and turning mind towards consecration—
Ne'er *was once*, but e'er our misery pulled by *Mercy's* play,
the birth-scent of this divine Power—Sweet as wild roses
as we drifted toward this foreign shore, struggling in sin's swell,
God's *Love* buoying us above the three strong currents of Hell,
saved from that tidal withdrawal the sensate mind imposes—
Beloved, *Let us love one another, for Love is of God*,
for in *Love* lies all certitude, all peace, all help for pain—
Joyful life of the *spirit's night*, this our contemplative rain,
sweet grace sounding on the will's highest ground—

THIS COVENANTED HEART

Yearning for your good *spirit*, the true *Image of God*,
cinder-like *spark* still burning once out of the *Center* brought,
from darkness unsound, this split masculine and feminine ground,
out of Mother Eve's *no pure* chaste virgin thought—
Now fiery eye reach to receive your *pure* Image of Light,
magnetic desire—on your Love's outflown unity feed;
Good and glowing *true spirit*— God's candle shining bright—
Soul in fiery nature *spirit* in Light's power, both decreed,
and your love's strength, precious life, only temple true—
Yet, if the soul's will to God's will submits *not* her desire,
you are dumb and dead, a mere mirror image vanishing soon,
even as a light flaming from a candle expires—
Holy genius— *idea* pure, a monstrous shape you assume
in horror, anguish, necessity and eternal despair,
and in body heat, cold, woes, sickness and a mortal life,
governed with greed, deceit, murder and pride's scarce repair,
by Satan's *spirit of error* ruled, mired spring of Man's strife—
But this cinder-like spark, still burning out of the *Center* bring
crushing error's spirit—killing self-will's love, of this we sing
to the *Holy Name Jesus*, great humility sublime,
Christ's soul and spirit in Love's essence, an open Gate attained,
Our true spirit *Idea*, God's *Image* renewed again—

THESE CRIMSON-BRUISED PETALS

Like a pleasant song
these crimson-bruised petals
For You live in the lauds of Israel—
Nothing else but
this understanding mind's essence,
this fire in your love-desire—
My great Ardent Longing arise
in this very dust of death—
Arise *Adonai* from
thy will's unsearchable
All—couching all things—
All creatures great and small
out of the hidden Earth's
delicate white Dogwood blossoms,
yet only *One* your ground—
O fiery Flame of Love desire!
They pierced my hands and my feet—
This sweet pleasing taste,
sweet-breathing scent,
ravishing melody
and lovely-delightful seeing—
For You have not hidden from me
your smiling and friendly face
when I cried to You—
Gracious delight and pleasure
now our mutual love-play

now wrestling one in another
this pregnant harmony—
Kingdom of Heaven's *Joy*—
Powerful all essential *Word*
King of Kings
You breathe forth
expressing your desire
and my heart is satisfied
in your queen Consort
coming forth from your wounded side—
Sophia sublime
like a pleasant song
these crimson-bruised petals—
For You have done this—

THE WOOD CHUCK

Come into this supra-imaginal ground—come and see,
overwhelmed and fainting spirit be set free—
Into phantasy's imaginary life once brought so low,
come forth where the wood chuck unwary quits its *Kennebec* den
putting off its bestial and feral to be friendly again—
Come to where the pink Taiwan lotus preens through its muddy
slough—
Lord, you have brought my spirit and soul out of the dark prison
to offer honour, praise and thanksgiving—to confess your *Name*,
living above images, figures, and shadows, now all tamed,
ruling o'er all creatures, this intellectual life's pure reason
receiving *no-thing* into my desire—from *all things* set free—
This child-heir prince of God reigning at once o'er all I see—

NOT SUSPECTED SUDDENNESS: *FEUERBLITZ* IV

As lightless as Laocoon's sons—this immortal soul,
so entangled and surrounded with the serpentine coil,
as trouble's dark web lay upon the surface of the *Deep*,
until *my* child learned to place this Cross upon the tree and weep—
Jordan's immersion moving upon the future man's heart—
Good, true and real light-bearing looking-glass from the start—
Sing my Soul
dancing shamelessly before the *Ark* of this open window:
"Come lightning—soft glimpse, the dark place of this heart winnow!
Scatter with your violent, yet silent 'Let the earth quake!'
Melt this cold hard saturnine salt; Christ's holy name invoke—
Astonish the bestial peacock dwelling in this astral part—
Put to silence the serpent encompassing this inward heart—
Come most effectual lightning stroke in this *dark night of grace*,
streaming white bolt dash this uroboros into the abyss."
Yet, my soul, rest not secure in this *Light is Sown*,
for the bane lies *just* exiled at your borders till the *Day* dawns—
So hie to the mountain of myrrh, to the hill of frankincense,
drawing out refined gold
both new and old unto Repentance—

VENUS ON NO HALF-SHELL: *THE GATES OF LOVE*

Venus on *no* half-shell, but nature's blessed kindler of *Love*—
Gracious proceeding from the *Heart-Son's* springing up,
this birth's surpassing sweet wine's lustre & o'er flowing cup,
You enthrall the Sun's fierce trembling with your meek *Light* from above,
as the lovely *Queen Anne's Lace* regales in the summer heat—
So *Venus*, your power makes fiery *Mars*— the fire crack, mild—
Jupiter's high-light and *Saturn's* hardness humble as a child,
as your innate *Love-Light* took the place of this world by the heart,
True Light sitting in the center of dark matter's spangled space—
For God would not let his Nature's body be benumbed in death,
nor his stretched-out Earth upon the plasmic waters be bereft,
where mighty Prince Lucifer sat ere his fall— this very place—
For out of the house of death—out of *this* lovely planet
your *fifth fountain's* pure and transparent *twelve* pearly *Gates of Love*,
your meek Seed, friendly affection, against the kindled waters strove—
O Dear *Love of Life*, that supposed lord You have supplanted—

THIS PURE CRAVING OURS

Stir this my spirit's desire
to wheel revolving within a wheel,
such a pregnant *flash of fire*
to go with it out of the fierce wrath—
Don't stop for Death, but dive down
into light's meek manifest inspire—
O Beauty of Colours!
Fully tasting one another—
Only satisfaction this pure craving ours
sprouting such peculiar fiery flowers
nothing but these pure virtues left,
three burning but joyous unfoldings
of *Majesty's light*, Love's own desire—
Once swollen soul now birth giving
to your first-born Image sublime,
here *eternal-time* is all your seeking,
all your desiring on which to dine—

FAIR AND FIERY SUNDAY

Hertz!
Joyful flash of the Lightning of Life—
Arise fair and fiery Sunday—swallow up this Saturn's night—
Shine in the terror of darkness—
of my soul cut off, become dumb and dead to my God Most High,
wandering as a wild beast wet with the dew of the heavens,
a beast to the Church, to the Holy Supper going in—
Eating it as an oxen on grass feeds—a beast coming out
standing hooved in this natural will—God's willing-spirit no more,
nor a new-born spirit, but from husk and history mere,
Release my spirit—
twenty years or more hearing sermons, receiving sacraments,
yet still the Devil's beast of vanity come out from thence—
For how can he partake who has no love or mouth of faith,
swelling in smug pride, ne'er by repentance humbled and abased,
venerating the shell—observing the form, but no kernel,
others assuming that *yoga* masters give life eternal,
Release my Soul—
struggling in vain with mantras to still imaginating minds,
some mocking with *Tartarean Twain* the harps of God sublime—
Some *go back to nature,* its outflowings their *avatars—*
the stars, Sun, Moon, and planets worshipping,
strumming their guitars,
so bestial Man weary and laden seeks his own absolution
crooning *love-is-love* with such bread and wine's *covened* abandon,
Release my true body—

transmogrified growing harpied hair and talon-like nails,
while *Rumi's* ribalds of Man's mineral evolution regale—
Unshriven scorners of the Holy Spirit's work, unbeseem—
Now arise fair and fiery Sunday with your redeeming beams,
from the Evil One who rules in the corruption of matter—
Return my Children—come out from this deceitful Moon's holy shows—
Go forth suddenly, Flash of Lightning give me understanding—
Blessings of praise, honour, and glory on the Most High bestow—

FALLING INTO THE BLESSED BIRTH OF LOVE

Open wide the *Gates of the Deep*
O kindled spirit—
Sparkle out of the eternal Mind
one pure virgin thought,
your fiery soul's desirous worthy,
the *will-spirit's* yearning to winged flight
to be reconceived, to be free
as a *Fire Bird*
out of the dark dust's ashes,
but cannot,
eternally desiring
but living like all the beasts
brazenly to four unholy horns bound,
an empty will-nothing but
quiet, death, and still
unknowing and terrified—
eternal, but standing in thick darkness—
O fixed infinity of the *Flash*,
but tethered to the Tree—
Tree of corrupting and corroding knowledge,
unable to break out of
this gyrating wheeling round
ever learning, but never simply satisfied,
ever conceiving to bear numberless fruits,

irrelevant species of stinging thoughts
insinuate into this interior ground,
so drawn and shut up within—

O great insufferable!
Come! O mystical death of my soul,
how zealously burning and thirsting to,
but not yet purified enough
beyond such violence to pass into my God—
To fall into the blessed birth of Love,
inwardly searching where and how
this one pure virgin thought—
Noble Body of perfect Wisdom,
beyond comprehension sweetly ravished
into this loving fiery *Crystal Sea*,
our simple sharing of Thy immensity—

UNBOUND

O my beloved companion
Chosen
to be *Unbound*—
When I take you to my bosom,
let the world do what it will,
only stay here with me
this little while
to bring your beautiful companions—
Brothers and sisters all
into my *Garden of Roses*
into this Lily of God
to show them my *Pearl*,
to come into my embrace,
till their wild beast breaks
and they abide here in my Heart
Unbound—

THEY SHALL NOT HINDER

These corrupters of the Earth,
so raging, so raving against your *Name* and Spirit Divine,
desecrating the golden vessels of your sanctuary,
besides themselves *at* this awakening grace which beckons
by whose *Light* they are at once astounded—
at the winter-blossoming Almond tossed into the pit,
the fiery Beacon shining 'neath the rain of stones,
Madame and her maid singing songs behind the Bastille walls,
the Lily-Rose's children exiled to the Nether Lands,
the fettered Watchman praying over his underground flock,
the alpine Peasant, alone, given to the black spider's blitz—
Yet, they shall not hinder
the blood of your Witnesses—
Blessed Seed of the Woman,
the Son which the old travailing mother brings forth,
Heaven declaring this
only holy kept *Sabbath* and Rest,
rest from mine own weary will and working,
as *You* draw me unto yourself,
as I turn and draw You,
the morning Dew giving itself to this deadened ground,
for my very own heavenly Virgin
hidden in the bounds of devouring Time,
confined high in the tower of this cold-hardened heart—
O let down your *Majesty's* flowing *splendour*
from the East unto the West—

For they shall not hinder
the Little Flock, here and everywhere,
your true *Mystical Body,* interior Temple of God,
chosen to be your Virgin Love-Child—

PLEDGE YOUR OWN HEART: A *PAEAN TO THE HOLY SPIRIT*

Pledge your own *Heart*, even your Light upon my soul,

though in my blinded sight, *Spirit*, You are as a No-Thing,

for not as quarks and phantasized infinities are You there;

And even these senseless stars have no knowledge of You,

though their seething plasmic waters flow forth,

cast into the *End of Greatness*, which these eyes cannot view,

though their motions in the tincture of our blood rise—

Pure *Spirit, Root* before the times this harsh world unfurled—

Winged quintessence hovering over this mind's dark *Chaos*,

pledge your own *Heart*, the life which *You* sent into this flesh,

highest earnest Witness saying, *I am the Light of the World*,

opening the deep *Gate of God* and the eternal birth,

exceeding pleasant, friendly, humble, and sweet,

O incorruptible bond of life—bottomless Depth

proceeding from the Father and his own *Heart-Son*,

laughing for joy as You spring up midst silent *Hallelujahs*—

Come most favorable *Fountain of Love* in the Fifth form,

pledge your own *Heart*—enkindle again this tongue of praise,

my soul from the loins of our Father's own substance sprung—

SWIFT AS A PURE THOUGHT MAGICAL

Where shall I go from your Spirit
when no place can bind such a thought?
Whether this soul abide in your *Dear Love*
or where every place is its Hell alike,
naked or clothed upon in this abyssal world,
my *Heaven* or my *Hell* everywhere,
though my spirit take flight,
go off a thousand miles
or a thousand times ten thousand,
this ten thousand times o'er,
even far past the *Great Attractors*
riding on the wings of dark energy's expansion,
knocking on the *End of Greatness'* door,
gliding through imaginary spaces beyond the stars—
Yet, You, *Adonai Sabaoth*, are still there—
O *my Splendour*, very same Infinity's *Point*,
still whence You had begun,
both near and afar-off all *One*,
be it in your Love or your Justice,
Abyssal Will altogether unconfined
aethereal passing through all things,
Swift as this pure though magical—

THIS TERRIBLE CONSUMING

Consume this essence of darkness,
this free *will* receive to Thy holy lips
sour wine with purging hyssop,
fair drawn light's desire bloom
out of the fiery life's dying
the lustre of the beauty of colours,
Love-desire's clear entreaty:
I thirst!
Only now the *Water of Life*—

THE CRICKETS

The crickets
their frenzied choral legs
keeping Esoteric Time
now stilled
at the whole World
in your *Hand*—
The reverential Awe!
O Possessor,
your unfathomable *Will*,
our Father *stirring*,
You grasp our seeds
while
possessing your *Heart-Son*—
Our place prepared,
and our tongues
too, fall dumb
at the *Wonder*—
O Separator divine
stand in the essence
of this your *likeness*
and speak to me
of *every thing beautiful*
wishing to be
about to be opened
in its own time
re-awakened

apprehended by that
immeasurable plumb
by which we apprehend
Ah! the Discovery—
Eternity set in our hearts,
the Apprehended One—

ANEMONE–

I've seen Thee, O gentle Crystalline Sea
with your myriad messengers
those fiery rowing sailors' flight
plying their *a-winged* oars with ease
through your balmy wonders perspicuously,
alighting here and there upon holy souls,
budding forth cherry blossoms white,
then gliding between those healing leaves
circumnavigating the *Tree of Life*,
regarding Emily's meek *Anemone*—

THE ORIOLE'S SONG

Our weariness is redressed
in the orange-breasted Oriole's song
as it dances upon the bough—
But your Sweet Love perceptible—
Eye of Seeing—
Ground of all beings,
willing always One
and only the same no-thing—

You who are not a being,
but only this Longing Delight,
still and quiet working of
not thinking, just pure intuiting
One Love who in pure Love
tenderly breathing births yourself
forth from yourself mobile:
Father, Son, and Holy Ghost—
O Lovely Assurgency
with your Wisdom manifest—
Imprinted Image of Joy this
ravishing delightful hearing,
this Magic Unfathomable
of Creation's primal place,
let my rapt soul now sing—
Yet your Sweet Love perceptible
deeper than any thought can plunge,
cannot be expressed—

I THEE ENDOW

I Thee endow,
Innocency's Virgin-Child,
this fiery love-desire
of my will freely give,
once so soon fooled away—
For I should have loved you
magically impregnating
our essences—
Your luminous *likeness*
out of my first *image*,
our one true self—
Tincture penetrating through
Love lubet's conceiving pair,
no longer bestial bodies *two*—
bare, miserable, naked,
but now *one* substance to share
His Majesty's Body—
Perfection dear
of your Venus's matrix,
love from the *Yield-Light World*
thrice drawing into
O Great Joy!
without pangs
without distress
magical birth-giving,
Rapt up pure no-thought—

Heaven's redress
to Thee I vow—

Verse Epilogue

FOR THE LILY'S SAKE

This high knowledge has not been striven for,
but we have only sought the *Heart-Son* of God
that we might hide us therein from the storm—
For when we entered in, the loving Virgin
out of the *Light-World* met us, proffered us her love—
She would be kind and befriend us,
be betrothed to us for a champion dear,
and show us the path to Paradise fair,
our safe haven from the stormy Tempest—
She carried a branch in her hand, beckoned and spoke—
Come, we shall plant this and a Lily will grow,
and I shall come to you again—
From whence we received this longing to write
of the amiable *Virgin Sophia's* way into Paradise,
as we sojourn in the kingdom of this world's night,
also, through the kingdom of Hell and no hurt done us—
So according to her directions we have written,
this hand penning deep mysteries at her bidding,
not from any advantages that can be counted on,
but for the children of Wisdom, the *Lily's* sake,
and for those who for the New Earth's *Yield-Light* long—

Endnotes/Sources

A Verse Dedication to the Reader:
I Want to Be Your Play Fellow
    SR Pref.
Introductory Poem:
A Coral Tree Grows in Gorlitz
    EP 10; *IN* 1.XII. 87–102
Poems of the Introduction:
Write, My Quill
    MM 5.14–15
I Only Sought the Pleasant Love-Heart
    EP XVII.6–12, 146–7
Thou Half-Dead Angel
    A 11.118–24
Lovely Candle
    TFL 1.17–19; *EP* 4.103–4; *EG* 2.50–61
Poetic Prologue:
A Sudden Shower
    EP 3.33–35, 54

SECTION ONE: *LILY*

A Good Friday, Falling
    IN 1.12.1: 2.7.48
My First Mother
    SR 14.6–7; *EP* 5.45–46; *EG* II; *A* 14.19–30; *A* 20

The Wind
 SR 2.39–40; *FT Explan*; *A* 7.43–45
The Rubied Cicada
 TP 15.38–39; *TFL* 11.32; *CL* 180–87; *A* 26.128–36; *TP* 10
My Dear Virgin
 IN 1.9.78–80
Hot Love Oil
 A 26.86–88,128–31; *WDI* 2.28–29
What Grace Is This?
 EG VII. 107–14
Hertz Is the Flash: *Feuerblitz* I
 TFL 3.23, 55–58; *SR* 11.69–70; *A* 8.128–38
Lovely, Gentle, and Still
 EG III. 22–30; *TFL* 3.13; *A* 20
He Shoots Up as a Lily
 IN 1.6.19–26
Spark
 FQ 1.139–46; *OTR* II.9–11; *STP* 3.IV.18; *EP* 32
Surrender, Falling
 IN 1.3.1–2, 5–14; *STP* 5.VII. 1–8; *A* 20
Flee Nakedly
 STP 3.IV. 18,21; *TFL* 16.7
Fruitful Rain in Your Still Mother
 TFL 16.1–9
Carmel Pacific *Gelassenheit*, March, 1973
 A 6.33–41
Shooting Forth Bright Into the Fair Lily
 STP Pref.
Descent Into the *Rakiya*
 MM 12.21–31; *A* 20; *FQ* 1.145,176; *EP* 6
Blade
 FT 1; *SR* 9.5–9; *TP* 12
Delight Draw Me
 FT 1 nos. 3–4; *FT* 2 (NN); *CL* nos. 172–6
Out of the Heart of Darkness
 IN 2.4.4–12; *TFL* 1.26; *TP* 14.65–80

SECTION TWO: *LILY-ROSE*

Blossom in the Time of the Lily-Rose
  SR 13.52; *EP* 9.1–15; *TP* 19.61;20.2, 12–14
Nights, Zion Downtown
  TFL 8.8; *A* 11.144–52
Once When I Was Yours
  IN 2.6.40–48; *A* 19.19–23
The Widow's Walk
  A 7.16–19; *SR* 1.15
You Know This Love Well
  A 19.9–23
Eagle: *The Inspoken Ungrund*
  IN 2.1.29–50; *TP* 22.20
The Hinge
  FQ APP.
No Mere Angel
  IN 1.5.107–15; *A* 14.28–31, 35
Married to a Beast
  MM 20.31–38; *IN* 1.7.9–28; *STP* 5.VII. 34–51
Stand Before the Crib Where Jesus Is Born
  TFL 3.25–34
Feuerblitz II
  TFL 3.22–23; *SR* 11.69–70
Know Thyself: *The Enemy Within*
  TP Pref.; *TFL* 14.12–56; *IN* 2.1.17
Burning Cold Night
  A 8.7–20; *TFL* 10.28–31
Pregnant
  WDI 3.7; *STP* 3.IV
Forked Lightning: *Feuerblitz* III
  STP 5.VII.1–32
This Rose Is Not a Rose Except
  EP 6.20, 36–61
As I Lay Upon the Mountain Towards Midnight
  TP 14.52; *IN* 1.7.39–44; *TP* 14.12

Miserere
>   *MM* 11.1–17; *SMP* Pref.; *OTR*: "A Prayer"

Pure Understanding Moon
>   *IN* 1.5.116–32; *EP* 16.4; 20.2

Bright Lily
>   *IN* 1.11.21–40

Signless
>   *WDI* 242–43; *FQ* App. 6–21

Know Thyself: *The Wild Heifers*
>   *TP* Intro; 3.8

Sapphire Dawn
>   *SR* 9.1–29; *TP* 14.1–12

Tender It the Love
>   *MM* 25.1–15; *TP* 20. 39 43, 53

A Terror of Great Joy
>   *TP* 12.43–50; 14.12–17; *TFL* 5.1–30, 144–45; *EP* 23.7; *IN* 2.4

Most Holy Sweet Power
>   *EG* 1.59–60; 6.76–77; 7.40–41

Lydia's Song
>   *EG* XII. 28–37; *EP* 23.12

Fire in the Iron
>   *TFL* 6.87–91, 97–103; *MM* 16.1–12

Rocking in the Cradle
>   *TFL* 6.33–40

Mother of Pearl
>   *TP* 9.31–32; *A* 26.86, 89

Pure Child
>   *STP* 1.2.9–10; 3.4.1–18; *A* 18.24–61

SECTION THREE: *PEARL*

Magus
>   *SR* 7.34–38; *EP* 5.76–88

Pearl
>   *MM* 10.22–24

Mary

IN 1.9.23–53
You Became Man for My Soul's Longing
    IN 2.6.40–54
Golden-Silver Child
    STP 1.2.9–10; *SR* 4.26–34; *SMP* 3
We Were Once Men and Women
    IN 1.11.28–70
Except for the Fair Paradisical Rose Garden
    MM 18.1–6
The Seraphic *Kadosh* of Wisdom: *A Food to the Divine Fire*
    TFL 10.28
My Being Is Your Moving in the Heavens
    IN 1.11.23–46
The Body Beautiful
    TP 13.1–14
Adam of the Crystal Sea
    TFL 5.127, 137–9
I Was Embraced With Love
    A 19.4–13
Rose Garden
    IN 1.7.16–60
One Love's Majestic Shining
    EG III. 42–48
Star-Dust
    TFL 1.1–16; *FQ* 33.19–20; *SR* 15.8
Dancing With Sophia
    SL (WTC CCEL) 24–25
Stand Still With Your Face Towards Me
    WTC (CCEL) *OTR* 25; *OR* nos. 50–55
The Time of the Lily
    TP 13.21–36
Riding in the Chariot of the Bride
    SR 69–79; *TFL* 16. 7–10; *TP* 13.28
Intimate and Indigenous
    FQ 6.20–25; *SR* 10.69–71; *TP* 13.28
That by Which God Saw and Heard in You

WTC (CCEL): *SL* Dialog 1; *FQ* 11–12
The Fellowship of His Sweet Interceding
    WTC (CCEL): *SL* Dialog 1; *WTC OTR* "The Gates"
The Thousandth
    FQ 6.20–25; *TP* 13.28; *EG* XIII. 41–48
Magia
    SMP 5.1–24; *FQ* 1.139–40
Iridium: *The Magical Begetting*
    IN 1.11.23–36
The Crystalline Silver Temple
    TP 10.2–11; *SR* 30–34; *MM* 16. 1–12; 18.1–9; *A* 21.30–51; *IN* 1.4. 25–42
Beloved Companion
    TFL 6.77–85; *IN* 1.12
The Yield-Light Constant
    TFL 3.16–18; *STP* 4.6.1–4; *A 19. 89–95*
The Doe
    STP 3.IV. 3–4
The Enchanted Bumble Bee
    SR XI.53–54; *TP* 19.12–20; *FQ* 22.1–22; *MM* 15–16.1–15
Upper Cross
    MM 10.25–26; *SR* Pref.; n. b.; *SR* 7.1–36;14.31–39
You Have Clothed the Naked
    WTC (CCEL) *SL* 10–25
Jupiter Sparkling Springing Up
    SR 14.33–35, 53; *TP* 12.29–30; 17.6–7; *A* 10.38–39, 55–63; 21.1–39
Chambered Nautilus: *Coming to the Limit*
    FQ 18.1–12; 21–22; *SMP* 5
The Pearl Is in the Jewel
    TP 9.45–47
Noble Burning White
    FQ 1.184–85; *IN* 2.6.40–43; *TFL* 1.26
These Great Moments: *On the Rebirthing of the Human Spirit*
    IN 1.5.1–17; *SMP* 6.1–2
Fire of God's Love Draw Me

WTC: SL nos. 45–47,52; *FQ* 21; *TP* 19
How Fair Now the Pine Trees of Lebanon
    TFL 11.112–13; 12. 10–11; *EP* 25.23–24; *EG* XIII.42–44
Set This Heart on Fire
    EG IX. 65–109
Pray Naked
    WTC: TR 43–45; *TP* 18. 58–59
High Life: *The Night Watch*
    WTC (CCEL): Dialog 2, nos. 120–22; *EP* 9. 31–38

SECTION FOUR: *JEWEL*

Love You Take All: *To the Noble Virgin*
    WTC: SL nos. 25–35
Out From the Very Heart: *A Mandala Shield*
    A 8.128–41
Soul Food
    IN 1.4.43–72
Outspoken
    A 16.10–15; *TP* 16.2–3
The Teacher
    EP 5.58–60
Come Forth Gently
    A 10.16–23
If Only My Spirit Did Sit in Your Heart
    A 9.17–37
The Scent of Wild Roses: *Reply to Arnold's Dover Beach*
    FT 2; *EG* II. 70
This Covenanted Heart
    FT 4 Explan: *IN* 1.12.1–6; *FQ* APP.
These Crimson-Bruised Petals
    MM 6.1–3
The Wood Chuck
    WTC (CCEL): *SL* pp. 104–5
Not Suspected Suddenness: *Feuerblitz* IV
    FT 3 Explan.

Venus on No Half-Shell: *The Gates of Love*
>   *A* 26.16–35

This Pure Craving Ours
>   *FQ* 1.141–54, 61

Fair and Fiery Sunday
>   *WTC: OR* VI. nos. 130–36; *FT* 4 Explan. n.p.

Falling Into the Blessed Birth of Love
>   *IN* 1.12.1–3; *TP* 16.1–5; *TFL* 1.24–26;3.1

Unbound
>   *TP* 21.58–64

They Shall Not Hinder
>   *EG* VII.107–17; *EP* 25.23–24

Pledge Your Own Heart: *A Paean to the Holy Spirit*
>   *TP* 4.18–41

Swift as a Pure Thought Magical
>   *WTC: SL* nos. 36–39

This Terrible Consuming
>   *SR* 14.12–13

The Crickets
>   *EG* I. 23–28; *EP* 6.54–67

Anemone
>   *FQ* 40

The Oriole's Song
>   *EG* I.41–63

I Thee Endow
>   *MM* 18.4–11; *SR* 3.8

VERSE EPILOGUE

For the Lily's Sake
>   *TFL* 3.5; *TP* 13.61;18.58

Bibliography

Bohme, Jakob. *The aurora.* Edited by C.J. Barker and D.S. Hehner. Translated by John Sparrow. London: J.M. Watkins, 1914. Item Link: Cornell University. http://onlinebooks.library.upenn.edu>lookupname.

———. *Concerning the election of grace. Or of Gods will towards man. Commonly called predestination . . .* Edited by Giles Calvert and John Allen. Translated by John Sparrow. London: J.M. Watkins, 1910. Item Link: University of California. http://onlinebooks.library.upenn.edu>lookupname.

———. *The epistles of Jacob Boehme.* Translated by John Ellistone (1649). Glasgow: John Thomson,1886. Item Link; Cornell University. http://onlinebooks.library.upenn.edu>lookupname.

———. *The forty questions of the soul, and The clavis.* Reissued by C.J.B. with emendations by D.S. Hehner. Translated by John Sparrow (1647). London: J.M. Watkins, 1911. Item Link: Yale University. http://onlinebooks.library.upenn.edu>lookupname.

———. *The high and deep searching out of the threefold life of man through : <or according to> the three principles.* Reissued by C.J.B. Englished by John Sparrow (1650). London: J.M. Watkins, 1909. Item Link: Yale University. http://onlinebooks.library.upenn.edu>lookupname.

———. *Mysterium Magnum. English.* With a Foreword ("To the Reader") and translated by John Sparrow. London: Henry Blunden, 1656; Text Creation Partnership. http://onlinebooks.library.upenn.edu>lookupname.

———. *The signature of all things, with other writings.* Translated and Preface by John Ellistone. London: J.M. Dent & Sons, 1926. Item Link: Indiana University. http://onlinebooks.library.upenn.edu>lookupname.

———. *Six theosophic points and other writings.* Translated by John Rolleston Earle. New York: A.A. Knopf, 1920. Item Link: Cornell University. http://onlinebooks.library.upenn.edu>lookupname.

———. *The three principles of the divine essence; of the eternal dark, light, and temporary world.* Translated by John Sparrow. Chicago: Yogi Publication Society, 1909. Item Link; Michigan State University. http://onlinebooks.library.upenn.edu>lookupname.

————. *The Treatise of the Incarnation: In Three Parts,* 1764. Translated by John Sparrow. in *Behmen's works,* edited by the Reverend William Law. London: M. Richardson, 1762–81. Item Link: Volume 2. Getty Research Institute. http://onlinebooks.library.upenn.edu>lookupname.

————. *The way to Christ, described in the following treatises: of true repentance, of true resignation, of regeneration, of the Supersensual life, written in the year* 1622. Canterbury: G. Moreton, 1894. Item Link: Yale University. http://onlinebooks.library.upenn.edu>lookupname.

————. *The Way to Christ* (multiple formats with commentary at CCEL). Item Link: Download. Christian Classics Ethereal Library. http://onlinebooks. library.upenn.edu>lookupname.